Until You Are Dead, Dead, Dead

Until You Are DEAD DEAD DEAD

The Hanging of Albert Edwin Batson

Jim Bradshaw and Danielle Miller

University Press of Mississippi / Jackson

www.upress.state.ms.us

The University Press of Mississippi is a member
of the Association of American University Presses.

Title page; Albert Edwin Batson. Photo reproduced from
Charles Dobson, Guilty? Side Lights on the Batson Case
(New Orleans, 1903), title page, no page number.

Manufactured in the United States of America

First printing 2014

∞

Library of Congress Cataloging-in-Publication Data

Bradshaw, Jim, 1944–
Until you are dead, dead, dead : the hanging of Albert Edwin Batson /
Jim Bradshaw and Danielle Miller.
pages cm
Includes bibliographical references and index.
ISBN 978-1-62846-099-5 (cloth : alk. paper) — ISBN 978-1-62846-100-8
(ebook) 1. Batson, Albert Edwin, 1881–1903. 2. Murder—Louisiana—
Case studies. I. Title.
HV6533.L8B73 2014
364.152'3092—dc23 2014014213

British Library Cataloging-in-Publication Data available

visiting the iniquity of the fathers
upon the children are sons of men.

publication supported by
Figure Foundation

To the memory
of Rachel Payne,
a stalwart,
loving mother

Contents

Preface

In the 1930s under the Works Progress Administration, John and Alan Lomax, the pioneering musicologists and folklorists, recorded early folk songs of Louisiana. One of those songs is a ballad about a man named Batson who supposedly killed six members of the L. S. Earll family on their farm in southwest Louisiana in February 1902. The song has more than thirty-five verses. Some of them are true to the actual story of the murder in an isolated farmhouse, but most are not; poetic license has been taken with most of the facts surrounding the case.[1]

The song and the case were forgotten by all but a handful of people, but in March 2008, John Newman of Nottingham, England, who was interested in American folk music, contacted the Genealogical and Historical Library in Lake Charles, the courthouse town for Calcasieu Parish (County), Louisiana. He'd come across a reference to the Batson ballad, had done a small bit of research on the song, and wanted to know more about it.

Danielle Miller, a genealogical research librarian, happened to be the person who answered his request. She found that the song was indeed based on a real event, but as she dug deeper, she also discovered many scrambled facts and unanswered questions about the case against Ed Batson, the man who was hanged for the murders—enough of them to cause her to begin to wonder whether there might be truth in the mournful refrain repeated between the verses of the ballad, "Oh, Mamma, I didn't done the crime."[2]

During Danielle's research she came across a reference to a newspaper column Jim Bradshaw had written for the *Daily Advertiser* in Lafayette.[3] She contacted him, and they collaborated on an hour-long PowerPoint presentation about the

Albert Edwin Batson. *Photo reproduced by permission from Catherine Todd.*

murders for the Lake Charles library. That presentation kept growing into this book.

Ed Batson was tried for and convicted of the murders twice (the first conviction was overturned by the state supreme court), sentenced each time to death, received a recommendation for commutation, but finally was hanged for the crimes. Law professor Richard Underwood, who did an extensive analysis of the case in 2007, called it "a classical circumstantial evidence case," and others have said it was "a classic case of mistaken identity."[4]

At the time of Batson's arrest, most of the citizenry of southwest Louisiana thought he was guilty. Sensational headlines in the local and the national press stirred enough emotion that there was genuine fear the accused man would be lynched, and also created a real belief on the part of some of the populace that a hanging would be the proper thing to do. But at least a handful of people—including two of the three members of the Louisiana pardon board—thought Batson was convicted on circumstantial evidence too flimsy to condemn a man to death and that the jury was already set against him when he finally went to trial.

It is impossible to recreate the mood of the times and to answer all the important questions as we come to this story more than one hundred years after the murders. Making the problem more difficult, few primary documents are left concerning the Batson case. We have searched in vain for trial transcripts at the district and appellate court levels. A Louisiana Supreme Court review after Ed Batson's first trial discusses specific pieces of testimony, but that information apparently came from attorneys' briefs and not a full transcript.[5] After Batson's second trial, members of the state pardon board said their decision was based on witness interviews because no full transcript of the trial was available. Any other documents that might have existed were destroyed in a disastrous fire in 1910 that leveled practically all the business section of Lake Charles, including the courthouse.

The greatest part of the research for this book comes from press reports at the time of the crime, long newspaper stories on Batson's two trials, and accounts of his ultimate execution. Those reports are inconsistent in the spelling of the names of several of the people and places involved. For example, the family name is variously spelled Earll, Earl, and Earle in newspaper accounts. We have elected to use Earll throughout the text, except in quoted matter. The name Lemuel is sometimes spelled Lemuell. We have chosen the single *l* because that is the way the name appears most often in print. Likewise, Maude Earll's name is sometimes spelled without an *e*, and Spickard, Missouri, is also written Spickards and Sprickard. We have chosen the spellings Maude, and Spickard, the name of the community as it appears on modern maps.

As might be imagined, we are indebted to a number of people who have helped us, most particularly, Shirley Burwell; Dot Akins; the staff of the Southwest Louisiana Genealogical and Historical Library; Beverly Delaney; Genevieve LeBlanc; Patty Shealy; Harold Hardy; Grace Dalton; Patti Threatt and Jan McFarlin of the McNeese State University Frazar Memorial Library in Lake Charles; Bruce Turner and Alvin Bethard of the Edith Garland Dupré Library at the University of Louisiana–Lafayette; Judy Cox of the Mercer County Library in Princeton, Missouri; the staff of the University of New Orleans Historical Library; the staff of the Law Library of Louisiana; John Newman in England; *History Detectives*, Lion Television in New York City; Nola Mae Ross; Janet Batson Davidson; John Garst; Joshua Caffery; Catherine Dunkin Stottlemyre Todd; Craig Gill and his helpful staff at the University Press of Mississippi; and especially to Josée Louise Minguet for her enthusiasm and encouragement; Randy Miller for his patience and support, and to Rose Marye Boudreaux for her many hours poring over the manuscript and making it infinitely better.

Jim Bradshaw
Danielle Miller

Until You Are Dead, Dead, Dead

Prologue

At about 1:40 P.M. on a steaming hot Friday, August 14, 1903, twenty-two-year-old Albert Edwin Batson stood quietly on the trapdoor that just minutes later would send him to his death. But Sheriff John Perkins, who was serving for the first time as an executioner, wasn't ready to pull the lever.

As he looked at the man who had been his prisoner for more than a year, the chief lawman of Calcasieu Parish in Louisiana realized he'd put the knot of the hangman's noose on the wrong side of Batson's neck. Batson and Perkins had been through a lot together, and the sheriff wanted this hanging done right.

Perkins had put the knot under Ed Batson's right ear; it was supposed to go under the left so it would break his neck when he fell through the open trapdoor.

"I ought to have put it on the left side," he told the prisoner.

"I believe it's all safe," the prisoner said.

Nonetheless, the sheriff moved the knot to the left side of Batson's neck.

As Perkins began to walk away, Batson stopped the sheriff and suggested that the noose should be a little more toward his ear.

The sheriff moved the rope, and then asked, "Are you ready?"

Batson did not answer until the trapdoor began to open. Then, just as he started to fall, he cried out, "Good-by."

Despite the sheriff's good intentions, the prisoner's neck did not break.

According to a report of his final hours, "Batson struggled for some time, and about twenty minutes after the drop fell the surgeons declared that life was extinct."[1]

From all appearances, Sheriff Perkins had grown to like the lanky, laconic young man he had to hang, even though two juries, the trial judge, the governor, and most of the people of southwest Louisiana believed Ed Batson brutally killed six people.

The Louisiana sheriff first became acquainted with the condemned man eighteen months earlier, when he went to Batson's hometown in Missouri where the accused killer had been taken into custody by local officials without any trouble. During a roundabout return trip to a jail cell in Lake Charles, the parish courthouse town, the sheriff had gone to great lengths to keep his ward from being lynched by citizens enraged over the gruesome, bloody murders he had been accused of.

The sheriff, who had seen Ed Batson almost daily for months and who perhaps knew him better than anyone else in southwest Louisiana, had not been called to testify when Batson went to trial. Some people said that was because the sheriff would have become a character witness for, not against, the defendant.

"The boy does not look like a murderer," the veteran sheriff had said when he first arrested him.[2] On Ed Batson's final day of life, the sheriff described him to the press as a model prisoner, soft spoken, obedient to the commands of his jailors, pleasant to be around.

Ed Batson said all along he never killed anyone. His mother said he couldn't have done the horrible killings because he was too squeamish at the sight of blood. But persuasive prosecutors and jurors willing to accept a train of circumstantial evidence thought otherwise, and innocent or guilty, Ed Batson went to his death for those murders.

The story began when he, or someone who looked like him, tried to sell some mules.

1

The Horse Trader

On Valentine's Day, February 14, 1902, about four o'clock in the afternoon, a man drove up to the stables of horse trader John Downs on Ryan Street, the main business street in Lake Charles, driving two sorrel mules pulling a rubber-tired buggy and leading two gray mules, a black horse, and a bay horse.[1]

The stranger, who had bartered unsuccessfully with another Lake Charles trader, J. Ed Ryan, over the stock earlier that day, said his name was Ward Earll and he was a rice planter from the little town of Welsh, thirty miles east of Lake Charles. He said he was giving up farming because his crop had failed, he was moving to Texas, and he wanted to sell the gray mules for $225.00.

The man was not Ward Earll. Ward Earll was dead in his bed in an isolated little house out on the southwest Louisiana prairie. Ward Earll's mother, father, and three younger brothers were also dead. All of them were brutally slain by the same killer or killers probably at the same time.

Authorities came to believe an itinerant worker named Albert Edwin "Ed" Batson committed those murders, largely because they believed he was the stranger who brought the Earll stock to Lake Charles. Batson had lived at Ward Earll's place and worked for him, but more than one hundred years later, questions linger on whether the right man was hanged.

The stranger who came to Lake Charles to sell the mules was at first described as a tall and slim man, weighing about 175 pounds. He was wearing a pair of overalls and calf-high rubber boots, commonly called gumboots. The horse trader particularly noticed a long scar on the left side of the man's face. The stranger told the liveryman he'd been farming near Welsh for several years but now was going to Texas "to grow corn and feed cattle."[2]

Downs said he would pay only $175 for the span of mules, and then only if Paul W. Daniels, a well-known businessman in Welsh, could identify the man and the mules. The stranger said that would be fine with him, and Downs told him to leave his horses and mules at the stable overnight. According to one account, the man decided to leave the mules but to take the horses with him; according to another, he left all the stock with Downs.[3] It is a point that is unclear in the existing record, but one that has some importance because Batson's accusers relied heavily on arguments over who had the stock and where the animals were kept.[4]

Before leaving the Downs stable on February 14, the man who called himself Ward Earll went to the buggy and appeared to write something on a piece of paper, which he placed in the pocket of a vest that he left in the buggy. Then he took from the buggy a double-barreled shotgun, which he said he was going to take to a gunsmith to have repaired, and a small square box that he said he wanted to send to Texas.[5]

Leaving the buggy at the stable, Downs used his own rig to drive the stranger to the Wells Fargo office several blocks away, but the men found it was closed. Then, by chance, they met Wells Fargo driver Orrin Mason on the street, and the stranger gave the box directly to Mason. However, the box was not addressed to someone in Texas, which is where the stranger told John Downs he was going to send it. It was addressed instead to Mrs. F. Joseph Payne, Ed Batson's mother, in Spickard, Missouri.[6]

After giving the box to the Wells Fargo driver, the stranger and horse trader went their separate ways. That was the last Downs saw of the man with the scar on his face until a month later when he was shown a newspaper photograph of Ed Batson, who by then had been accused of the horrendous murders and was under arrest for them. John Downs identified Batson as the man who'd come to his stable on February 14 and tried to sell him Ward Earll's stock.

Left behind in the stranger's wagon at Downs's stable were the business card of a man named Harris, two packages of tobacco, an alarm clock, three keys, a bottle of ink, a pen holder, a spool of black thread, a pocket comb, a gray vest, and parts of a letter from Ed Batson's mother.[7]

There was also a curious letter dated December 19, 1901, two months earlier, which read:

> P. D. Plantation
> Welsh, La.
>
> To any one whom it may concern thereof. I one, Edwin Batson, hereby giving my signature to this date, give my whereabouts to the public or to anyone who finds this slip of paper my name as follows Albert Edwin Batson was born in Atchison Mo Apr 8 1881 my father and M John and J Batson lived in said places J my father lives in Nodoway Co. Mo my mother being now Mrs. Joe Bayne [*sic*] lives in Spickards Mercer Co Mo my sister Mrs C M Vredenburg lives in Princeton Mercer Co Mo my brother J. N. Batson I do not know where he is but he that finds this will do the dead justice by sending my mother or my sister word of my death, and how it occurred. This is all I request of the dear friends. So a long and happy life I do wish to you all
> Signed a rit x—2..y/l-fare well [*sic*]
> A. E. Batson
> friend to all. Ha ha bye bye I'm gone[8]

Authorities later referred to this as the "Ha-Ha Letter" and tried to use it to connect Ed Batson to the murders. They claimed the letter showed he was contemplating suicide, but they never gave a reason why he didn't kill himself if that was his intent.[9]

2

Scene of the Crime

When the man who brought the stock to John Downs's livery stable agreed to leave some mules to be identified by Welsh businessman Paul Daniels, he asked how soon Daniels could be there to look at them. He was told that Daniels could probably come to Lake Charles on the train that evening.[1]

But, inexplicably, it wasn't until four o'clock in the afternoon on February 24, ten days after the stranger had left the mules with Downs, that the horse trader finally telephoned Daniels and told him he was holding some stock left there by a man who said he was Ward Earll of Welsh.[2]

That didn't sound right to Daniels, and he called Maude Earll, Ward's sister, who was working in the A. E. Bell general merchandise store in Welsh and living in town with the Bell family. She was already a bit uneasy because she had not heard from her parents or siblings in several days, and Daniels's call made her even more so. She hired a buggy from Petre's Livery in Welsh and a driver named Bill to take her to the family farm to see what was what.[3]

It was almost dark when Maude and the driver got to the rundown house Ward Earll shared with his hired worker Ed Batson on the Old Spanish Trail about two miles west of Welsh. The small house was about a half mile south of the Southern Pacific Railroad track and visible from passing trains, but stood alone on the prairie almost a mile from the nearest neighbor.[4] It was closer to Welsh than a second house that was about a mile west on what is now LeBlanc Road and was occupied by Maude's father, mother, and younger siblings.[5]

This depiction of Ward Earll's cabin appeared in the *Houston Post*, "Batson Is on Trial," April 15, 1902, 3.

The front door to Ward Earll's house was locked, and the windows were barred, but Maude and Bill were able to enter the house through a rear door that opened into a living room. Nothing seemed unusual at first, but there was a distinct foul odor.[6]

Maude went through the living room and across a central hallway, past the foot of a stairway leading to an attic room, and tried the door of her brother's bedroom. It seemed to be blocked by something. When she finally pushed it partly open and looked inside, she "fell fainting into the driver's arms," according the first lurid press accounts of the murders. She had glimpsed the bodies of her brothers and mother "piled like cordwood" in the little bedroom.[7]

"Without permitting the girl to examine [the scene] further, the driver carried her to the buggy and drove on a run to Welsh," according to the Lake Charles press. "A small party of men accompanied him back to the cabin and found the little room full of corpses." The bodies "had already become greatly decomposed," showing "plainly" that the family had been murdered days, if not weeks, earlier.[8]

Fifty-five-year-old Lemuel Sheldon "L. S." Earll, the patriarch of the family, was not found in Ward's house or his own a mile or so down the road. Officers presumed he also was dead, a presumption turned into fact at daylight the next morning when he was found half buried in a ditch near his house, shot dead.[9]

The only members of the family left alive were Maude and her brother Fred, who was said to be living with an uncle in Eagle Grove, Iowa, although census and other records do not confirm that.[10]

Newspapers gave vivid descriptions of the gory scene found in Ward Earll's sixteen-by-sixteen-foot bedroom: "[Mrs. Earll] had the whole front of her face mashed in with some blunt instrument. One of her sons [Ward] had been shot through the head and the throats of two others had been cut."[11]

According to first accounts in the *Lake Charles Weekly American*,

> The way the bodies lay when they were found indicated that the murders were committed in daylight. Ward Earle, the oldest son, was probably the first victim. He was apparently lying in bed, fully clothed, and was probably murdered while he slept. It was supposed [his younger brothers] were sent over one by one from the family home. The murderer lay in wait and killed them as they came, shooting them, crushing their heads, then cutting their throats, and laying their bodies on the floor. [Ward's mother] was next and was beaten to death; her head was all crushed in. The murderer then went to the other house . . . and killed [Ward's father].[12]

The coroner later testified that Ward, who was twenty-five years old, had probably been shot while he was asleep by someone using a shotgun loaded with No. 3 or No. 4 shot. His wound was in the left eye. Seventeen-year-old John was shot in the spine; nineteen-year-old Fay in the left ear. Thirteen-year-old Lemuel, nicknamed "Lemmie," and Mrs. Earll were each battered in the face with a blunt instrument, possibly the butt of a shotgun.[13]

The first newspaper accounts described the house as being "in perfect order," except that a drawer filled with papers had been emptied on the table. There was no evidence of a struggle, but pieces of clothing and the contents of a trunk that was found open in the room were scattered around.[14] Later reports described walls "filled with shot" and empty cartridge shells strewn about.[15]

Records showed that John and Lemmie had been absent from school for ten days before the discovery of the bodies; the Earlls' mail had accumulated in the Welsh post office for at least a week; and Maude had not seen any of her family for ten days—all of which led Calcasieu Parish corner Thomas Henry Watkins to believe the murders took place on February 13, the day before the man with the mules and horses showed up in Lake Charles.[16]

Near the house, the first investigators found a signed note that apparently had been tacked to the door of the cabin but had been blown into the yard. Four tacks were still stuck to the door. The note said Ward had gone to Lake Charles and would return in several days. They found scraps of paper inside the house with parts of the same note written out, as though someone had been practicing handwriting.[17]

Lawmen said two men had stopped at the house on Saturday, February 8 (five days before the alleged date of the killing), saw the note on the door, and left without trying to enter. They also said at first that a tramp had been seen hanging around the area "for some time" and that he might have had a hand in the killings, but they later decided he had not.[18]

Investigators also found an old horse that died of starvation in the barn at the L. S. Earll place, the main farmhouse about a mile away, and a mule tied to a China ball tree that had apparently survived by eating the bark off the tree. The stock taken to Lake Charles and the two animals left behind constituted about a third of the stock usually kept on the Earll farm. The rest of the stock was gone, and that became a point even in the shadow of the gallows that Ed Batson argued helped prove his innocence. "Find who took the rest of the stock and you'll find the murderer," he maintained until his dying day.[19]

Another trunk was found open and appeared to have been rifled at L. S. Earll's main farmhouse. A piece of cloth was still in a sewing machine in the kitchen, as if someone had been sewing and was suddenly interrupted. Also, a drawer filled with papers had been emptied on a table.[20]

3

Coroner's Inquest

Reports conflict about the state of the crime scene when authorities began their investigation. Underwood writes, "Unfortunately, a crowd gathered quickly, and the bodies were moved before the coroner could get to the scene. This, and the limited nature of the sciences of the day, made a modern and thorough forensic investigation impossible."[1]

However, the *Lake Charles Weekly American* reported on March 1, "Citizens kept watch over the house of such evil happenings and when Coroner Watkins reached the scene . . . nothing had been disturbed except the door leading to the room where the bodies were found. It was necessary to break this from its hinges to gain an entrance."[2]

Whichever the case, Watkins quickly assembled a five-man panel of Earll neighbors and held an inquest to try to sort out what had happened in the forlorn little house on the prairie. These men found that the Earlls had died at the hands of "parties unknown . . . probably . . . Batson." The panel—called a *coroner's jury* in legal terms—took note that "a tramp had been hanging around in that locality" but also came to the conclusion that "one man alone was guilty of the six-fold murder," despite having used the plural phrase "*parties* unknown" earlier in its report.[3] Jurors examined "every possible scintilla of evidence . . . that could shed light on the tragedy," according to the press. Maude Earll did not testify because "since she caught a glimpse of the frightful sight . . . [in] Ward Earll's dwelling place, she [has] been hysterical and half-demented."[4]

The authorities who forced the bedroom door open found a frightful sight—Lemmie and John sprawled on the floor with their feet against the door and their mother, Mary, lying atop them. Their brother Fay's remains were in a corner of the room; Ward was on the bed, "in a natural position, as if sleeping." He was dressed in the clothes he might have worn to town, not in work clothes. Fay had a load of shot through the back of the neck. The mother's face from the lower jaw had been bashed or perhaps shot away. The youngest son, Lemmie, had been struck from behind with a blunt weapon, crushing his skull and breaking his neck.[5]

And then, "to make sure of his work, the unspeakable wretch who did the deed, had drawn a knife across the throat of each of his victims, severing each from ear to ear." Cloth was wrapped around the neck wounds, presumably by the killer.[6]

Newspaper writers speculated that the cloth was meant to stop bleeding from the wounds, but quite often there is little bleeding associated with even severe wounds inflicted after someone is already dead. In fact, the *Lake Charles Weekly American* reported in one of the first descriptions of the crime scene that "little blood was on the floor and none in the rest of the rooms."[7]

Even as investigators began to focus on Ed Batson as the killer, questions began to arise about why he would have done such a thing. In the *Signal*, published in Crowley, another small farming community about twenty miles east of Welsh, the reporter wrote, "Batson's motive for wiping out the Earll family is a mystery unless it was for getting hold of the mules [which] is [too] preposterous for belief. If he had any grudge against the Earlls, or any one of them, it is not known here and his tigerish thirst for blood is beyond understanding. Some are inclined to think the man became insane, being unable to believe he could have butchered his victims as he did had he been in his right mind."[8]

Investigators said the motive for the murders was money. The Earlls were described as "well to do people" who had lived nearly twenty years in Louisiana and who owned their 640-acre rice farm. The family had just sold nine hundred sacks of rice, and the money from that sale was at first thought to be in the house.[9]

Dr. T. H. Watkins, Calcasieu Parish coroner in 1902. *Photo courtesy of the Archives, Frazar Memorial Library, McNeese State University, Lake Charles, LA.*

But that motive was discounted when authorities found two thousand dollars from the sale of the rice safe in the bank in Welsh. Another five hundred dollars of the proceeds had been used to pay a debt, leaving "possibly a few hundred dollars" to be gained by a crime, which in at least one reporter's view, "for devilish cunning and cold-blooded ferocity, is unparalleled in the history of Louisiana and . . . unique in the annals of crime."[10]

The *St. Louis Republic* reported later that "close estimates" by Ward's surviving brother, Fred Earll, indicated that $115 was missing from the two Earll houses. "On Wednesday Ward Earl gave John a check for $25 to cash," according to that report. "The boy got the money and, after paying a few small bills and buying some few things, had $30 [*sic*] left, which he intended to bring to Ward. Mrs. Earl always carried from $80 to $90 about her person. She never allowed the amount to go below $80. This money she must have had on the afternoon of the murder. The money was not on hand [when the murders were discovered]. Mr. Earll always carried around $5, and this money was also gone."[11]

The *Republic* reporter did not speculate about how Fred Earll, who was supposedly hundreds of miles away in Eagle Grove, Iowa, knew about Ward Earll's transactions with his younger brother John and the amount of money Mr. and Mrs. Earll were carrying. The statement that the boy had $30 left was probably a typographical error, since the check he was given to cash was only for $25.

The coroner's investigation also did not resolve the questions of just when the murders had been committed. Neither Ward Earll's house nor the family farmhouse were on well-traveled roads, "and this, coupled with the fact that the family kept to themselves generally and had not been residents of the neighborhood for a great while, accounts for the delay in discovering the crime," according to one Lake Charles newspaper.[12]

One neighbor said he'd seen Ward and his father working in the fields on Monday, February 10, but the field where he said they were plowing seemed to be undisturbed, and two men who went to Ward Earll's house on February 8 said they found a note saying he'd gone to Lake Charles. Their teacher said the younger brothers, Lemmie and Fay, had been in class on Wednesday, February 12, but that neither of the schoolboys had been present since February 13.[13]

"Taken in connection with Batson's appearance at Downs's February 14, the inference is plain that the crime was committed the evening of [February 13]; that it was perpetrated before dark is apparent from the fact that all were fully clothed except for Ward, who had his coat and vest off," according to newspaper speculation.[14]

However, the St. Louis newspaper reported on March 25 that "careful study of the details of the murders" showed that the Earlls were killed on February 12, not February 13.

> Mr. Fred Earl . . . is of this opinion, and gives very strong reasons for believing that way. . . . He thinks that Ward Earl was shot in the early afternoon or in the morning when asleep. Every indication points to that fact, and that Fay Earl ran into the room to learn the cause of the shooting and was himself

> shot down. The two boys [Fay and John] certainly stopped at Ward Earl's house on their way home from school. They both rode John Earl's pony and turned it loose.
>
> The animal at once wandered home, and [Fred] . . . believes that his mother became frightened at the riderless pony and at once walked over to Ward's house to learn the trouble. [Fred] believes [that L. S.] was out in the field, just in the act of returning to the house, when Batson came upon him and shot him down.[15]

Another question the inquest failed to ask or answer was how the killer got out of the room. The killer had to be inside the room when the bodies were stacked against the door in such a way that it could not be opened. Maude Earll and the livery driver found the windows to the room barred and covered with oilcloth so they could not get in or see into the room. With the door blocked and the windows barred, how did the killer get out of the room?

Calcasieu deputies sent telegrams to authorities across the country "to look out for suspicious characters," but "the whole suspicion," the *New Orleans Picayune* reported, "seems to point to Ward Earll's hired man . . . [who] by the description given by the mule dealer in Lake Charles . . . is the same man, as he had an ugly scar on the right cheek."[16] Batson did have a scar on his right cheek, but according to the press, the mule dealer Downs at first described a man with a "long burnt scar" on his left cheek.[17]

The Lake Charles newspaper described the hired man, Batson, as "about 25 years old, weighing about 150 pounds, about 5 feet 9 inches tall, hair between brown and black." But liveryman John Downs told the same newspaper that the man who brought mules to his barn was tall, slim, and weighed about 175 pounds.[18] He had been employed by the Earll family for about eight months, before that working at a pumping plant used to irrigate rice fields south of Welsh. According to the news account, Batson "had several quarrels while there and was looked upon as a bad character."[19]

The account also noted that Batson "had a scar over his right eye, which curves down in a circle on his face in the shape of a horseshoe," and "is so plain that it will make his identification very easy."[20] When Maude Earll heard that the man who brought the mules to Lake Charles had such a scar on his face, she immediately concluded that it was Ed Batson, adding weight to the belief by the coroner and the sheriff that he was the murderer.[21]

It apparently went unremarked that the horse trader John Downs had said the man who brought the mules was scarred on his left cheek, not the right, and at first he described a man heavier and taller than the man described as Batson in the newspaper. It was also significant in the eyes of the law that, like the Earlls, Batson had not been seen in the area for a week or more.

Telegrams sent to law enforcement agencies by Calcasieu Parish authorities gave a full description of Batson and called for his detention. They put a one-hundred-dollar bounty on his head, and Calcasieu Parish chief deputy sheriff Charles M. Richard also wired Louisiana governor William Heard, asking for "a suitable reward" for Batson's arrest.[22]

Meanwhile, as her family was prepared for burial, Maude Earll remained in a "critical" emotional state. The *Crowley Signal* reported on March 1 that she "may not survive the shock" and "seems dazed to all surroundings and it may result in her mind becoming permanently imbalanced."[23] The scene on the day of the funeral was dramatically described by the *Weekly American*.

> Up the little streets of Welsh . . . passed the most pathetic procession human eye ever rested upon in Calcasieu Parish. Ahead rode Rev. S. W. Turner, of the Presbyterian church; next came two drays bearing the battered remains of the Earll family, butchered by the fiend Batson. Five of the caskets were enclosed in large pine boxes and the sixth box was partially open, permitting a glimpse of a white coffin containing the remains of little Lemmie, the "baby" of the family. A few carriages containing

> sympathizing friends made up the balance. . . . Prevented by physical weakness from seeing the last of her loved ones, Miss Maud's only request was that the funeral procession should pass [her employer's] home [where she lived] on its way to the cemetery. Accordingly, the melancholy cortege made a detour down the main street, while the citizens of Welsh looked on, still numbed by the shock of the tragedy, and passed on to the cemetery, where in one immense grave the bodies of Batson's victims were laid to rest.[24]

At that time the "fiend" Batson had not been arrested or questioned. But the papers still reported that the Earlls had been "Batson's victims."[25]

4

Cajun Prairies

Funeral corteges for people who died violent deaths were not wholly unusual in Welsh in the early 1900s and the decades before. In fact, the very house where Ward Earll and his mother and brothers were found murdered already had a history of violence. A Calcasieu Parish police juror (county official) even speculated that the Earll murders may have been the work of a madman who returned to the same house regularly.

According to a *Washington (DC) Times* article written the day testimony began in Ed Batson's first trial:

> Mr. Arceneaux, police juror of Calcasieu, today brought out the fact that in the very house in which the Earl family had been murdered another family had been similarly murdered ten years ago. The crime was equally bloodthirsty and unnecessarily brutal, but no trace could ever be found of the murderer, and the theory was entertained by many that the murderer was a homicidal maniac.
>
> Not only that, but some years later a boy had been murdered in the house and the crime had remained undiscovered. Mr. Arceneaux's idea is that both sets of crimes were committed by a madman who returned years afterward to the house where he had killed the first family and in similar manner murdered the Earls.[1]

Arceneaux suggested that the very "fiendishness" of the murders was Batson's strongest defense: "The murder of the little boys and mutilation of the slain seemed . . . incompatible with a well-mannered young man of twenty-two."[2]

Journalist Charles Dobson, who wrote a book defending Batson, said the little house had once been occupied by a homesteader who made a few improvements to the land, then suddenly went away for eighteen months. When he returned, he found that his right to homestead the property had been overturned on a legal technicality, and another man was now homesteading there. According to Dobson's account, published in his book in 1903,

> Fourteen years ago a party of small boys, blackberry-hunting, sought rest under the shade of a tree situated upon this homestead. The balmy breeze common to the Gulf coast they soon realized was poisoned with the odor of decayed flesh, for which they searched and discovered the body of a man. It was . . . the second homesteader. A hole in the skull showed that death resulted from a pistol-shot wound. By his side lay a pistol which led to a theory of suicide, but discerning men did not accept it, for upon the shirt sleeve of the left arm were bloody finger prints of a left hand; this circumstance showed that some other person was present while the lost blood was still fresh. The mystery of the man's death is yet unsolved.[3]

According to Dobson, about three years later a cattle buyer from Texas was caught in a rain shower as he approached the small house. When he went into the house to get out of the rain, "he was met with the sight of the bleeding body of a boy, terribly wounded, who expired almost immediately. . . . The boy [was] identified as a neighbor's son. Strange to say, this boy's father had aided homesteader No. 2 in the contest of claims. . . . The mystery of this boy's death is unsolved."[4]

At the time of the Earll murders in February 1902, Calcasieu Parish encompassed some 3,600 square miles, an area more than twice the size of Rhode Island. It still had some of the character of the western frontier in the days after the Civil War, but it was also beginning to get the smell of money in the air. Some people say these prairies where L. S. Earll and his family came to settle were the birthplace of the American cattle industry. The region was certainly referred

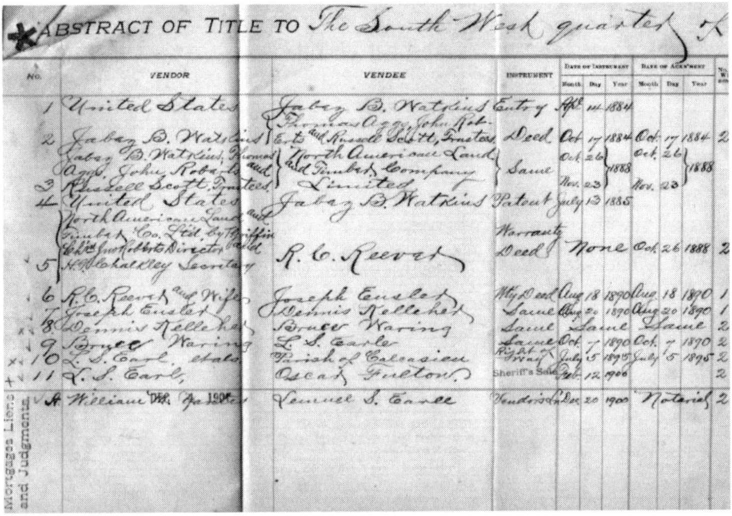

ABSTRACT OF TITLE TO The South West quarter of

No.	Vendor	Vendee	Instrument	Date of Instrument (Month Day Year)	Date of Ack'ment (Month Day Year)	
1	United States	Jabez B. Watkins	Entry	Apl 14 1884		
2	Jabez B. Watkins	Thomas Ogg, John Robt. and Russell Scott, Trustees	Deed	Oct 17 1884	Oct 17 1884	2
3	Jabez B. Watkins, Thomas Ogg, John Robt. and Russell Scott, Trustees	North American Land and Timber Company Limited	Same	Oct 26 1888 / Nov 23 1888	Oct 26 1888 / Nov 23 1888	
4	United States	Jabez B. Watkins	Patent	July 13 1885		
5	North American Land and Timber Co. Ltd. by [illegible] Director and [illegible] Secretary	R. C. Reeves	Warranty Deed	None	Oct 26 1888	2
6	R. C. Reeves and wife	Joseph Ensley	Wty Deed	Aug 18 1890	Aug 18 1890	1
7	Joseph Ensley	Dennis Kelleher	Same	Aug 20 1890	Aug 20 1890	1
8	Dennis Kelleher	Bruce Waring	Same	Same	Same	2
9	Bruce Waring	L. S. Earle	Same	Oct 7 1890	Oct 7 1890	2
10	L. S. Earl, et als	Parish of Calcasieu	Right of Way	July 5 1895	July 5 1895	2
11	L. S. Earl	Oscar Fulton	Sheriff's Sale	Feb 12 1906		2
A	William [illegible]	Samuel S. Earle	Vendor's Lien	Dec 20 1900	Notarial	2

Mortgages Liens and Judgments

This handwritten abstract traces the ownership of L. S. Earll's farm (transaction 11) to the original ownership of entrepreneur J. B. Watkins. *Reproduced by permission of Warren and Genevieve LeBlanc.*

to by settlers and travelers in the late 1700s as "cow country" because of huge herds of cattle found grazing there. But until the railroads arrived in the 1880s, the French-speaking descendants of the Acadians, or Cajuns as they are popularly known today, and others who settled the area lived on the eastern and western fringes of the prairies or along the streams that ran through them where they could find amenities such as firewood, which was a scarce commodity on the treeless grassland.[5]

By the early 1800s cattle meant big business in southwest Louisiana. Lawyer, writer, and explorer Henry M. Brackenridge reported in 1814, "The number of cattle composing the herds which some of the wealthier possess would in other parts of the United Sates be considered incredible; there are several who market from one to two thousand calves a year. The cattle driven to New Orleans for sale bring fifteen to twenty dollars a head."[6]

But after the Civil War the cattle industry began to falter because of a fever brought in by Mexican beef—just about the time the railroads spanned the prairie, and land agents began to seek farmers from the Midwest to grow crops, not cattle, on the sparsely settled, fertile prairie.

Then, just at the turn of the century, drillers found rich oil deposits not thirty miles from L. S. Earll's home. That brought speculators, roughnecks, and young men like Ed Batson, who found themselves traveling the country, stopping wherever a good job could be had.

Protestant English-speaking midwesterners such as the Earlls began to move next to the Catholic French-speaking Cajuns in the middle 1800s and found that the land was ideal for rice culture.[7] That, among other things, set up a rivalry between old cattlemen who had allowed herds to roam the prairies freely and the new rice growers who fenced their land to keep cattle away from lush, tempting fields. The conflict sometimes festered into open hostility simply because the newcomers, *les américains*, and the Cajun cattlemen did not understand—or want to understand—the other's language or culture.

Historians such as Donald Millet Sr., whose important studies focused particularly on the economic history of southwest Louisiana, credit a handful of people with providing the first impetus to widespread prairie settlement. They included, among others, Jabez Bunting Watkins, a land speculator and dreamer, whom Millet describes as an "entrepreneur in the age of enterprise"; Seaman A. Knapp, an "educator who taught the farmers the value of experimentation and demonstration"; and Sylvester L. Cary, "land agent for the Southern Railroad Company, who induced thousands of Midwesterners to seek their fortunes in the prairies of Louisiana." Largely because of such farsighted men, the prairie region population more than doubled between 1880 and 1900, from 76,572 to 154,024.[8]

Cary, a New York native who moved to Iowa in 1853, lured hundreds of families to southwest Louisiana after he discovered the rich prairie lands ripe for the plow. He moved to the newly organized town of Jennings in 1883 as station agent for Southern Pacific, and the next year became the northern

J. B. Watkins. *Photo courtesy of the Archives, Frazar Memorial Library, McNeese State University, Lake Charles, LA.*

immigration agent for the company, touring Iowa and Illinois to recruit farmers to settle in Louisiana and, presumably, ship their crops to market by the railroad that brought them there.[9] He told his friends in Iowa there were five million acres of marsh and overflowed land that could be bought for twelve cents an acre. Another three million acres were available under the Federal Homestead Act of 1862 in 160-acre patches for as little as fourteen dollars down and the payment of another nine dollars at the end of five years.[10]

Farmers who heard Cary's pitch became even more interested when a dry summer and severe winter in 1886 and 1887 all but wiped out wheat crops in the Midwest. They decided to accept the railroad's offer of a free ride to Louisiana, bringing with them implements that would serve to plant, tend, and harvest rice in south Louisiana as well as they did for the wheat grown in the Midwest. By 1893 "Cary's Iowa Colony" in Louisiana was flourishing, and so were its rice crops.

British capital financed the land boom once the railroads opened the prairie. The London-based North American Land

and Timber Company swallowed up 1.5 million acres of land in what is now four parishes, paying twelve cents an acre for marshland and as little as seventy-five cents an acre for prairie. On behalf of the company, Watkins bought the property that would become the Earll farm in 1884, about the same time the railroad began to aggressively promote the prairies.[11]

Watkins, who became the North American Land and Timber Company agent in Louisiana, had been a banker in Lawrence, Kansas, but now showed himself as one of the most enterprising promoters ever to hit Louisiana. He thought southwest Louisiana's rich wetland soil could be used to grow rice if the marshes bordering the prairie in coastal Louisiana could be drained and the water kept out with levees.

Beneath these marshes, he thought he would find a "rich, black vegetable mold, six feet deep, possessing a fertility unsurpassed in the world," and that once it was drained it would make a perfect soil for rice. He planned to bring people from Holland who had experience with lowlands to build levees and dikes that would allow the wetlands to be pumped dry to create a Garden of Eden for rice growers.[12]

He tried to raise capital in the United States to fulfill his dream, but no one believed in him, so he went to England to get the money, which he used to buy huge tracts of what others considered wasteland.[13]

The rice venture failed in the lowest parts of the marsh where too much salt in the water caused the crops to die. Watkins built his levees by stacking marsh mud on top of marsh mud, but saltwater seeped right through, poisoning the rice crop. On higher ground, where the rice was irrigated with freshwater, the results were hugely successful and made a fortune for Watkins and his business partners.[14]

One of the reasons for his success was that Watkins realized he needed not only the land, but the farmers to till it. He bought a newspaper in New York to publicize his vision of a bountiful south Louisiana and later moved the publication to Lake Charles, where it became the forerunner of the *Lake Charles American Press*, which is still being published. He outfitted a railroad car with Louisiana products and land company brochures and toured the Midwest. When yellow fever and malaria scares threatened to keep settlers away, Watkins organized the Telegraph Medicine Company to advertise and sell an antimalaria patent medicine.

He made an offer to "the ten first acceptable applicants" of up to 230 acres of land, within five miles of the railroad at five dollars per acre, with eleven years to pay for the land. As an additional incentive, the land company would give settlers fencing materials, twenty-five mares, twenty cows, ten brood sows, and fifty ewes and provide for breeding of the animals with the best stock available. An "acceptable applicant" had to be "an experienced and energetic farmer, honest, industrious and temperate. . . . worth $1000 or more, and [with] plenty of help in his own family to do all the work."[15]

L. S. Earll and his family were among the many midwesterners who were captivated by the evangelizing of Watkins and his cohorts. Earll had moved from New York State to Iowa at least by 1870, when his family was counted there in the federal census. According to the 1900 census, they were living on their farm near Welsh, apparently making a decent living using what amounted to revolutionary rice farming techniques.

Almost from the first settlement of the prairies, Cajuns had grown what they called *providence* rice by broadcasting some rice in a wet place and letting providence take its course. But Millet and others say the first truly large commercial rice crops began in southwest Louisiana with the midwesterners and particularly with the adaptation for the rice harvest in 1884 of a machine called the twine binder that had been used in the Midwest during the wheat harvest. Invented by Cyrus McCormick, the binder was used to tie the top shocks of wheat (or rice) together for easier harvesting and handling.[16] Mechanical rice harvesters were introduced only a few years later.[17]

Rice production soared after introduction of this technology. Farms increased in size from a few acres in the early 1880s to hundreds and thousands of acres by the end of the decade. The Southern Pacific Railroad shipped about 250 cars of rice from prairie farms in 1884; over 1,000 in 1889; 2,000 in 1890; 5,000 in 1891; and for 1892 and 1893, 10,000 cars.[18]

Because growing rice requires a lot of water, huge irrigation projects aided the cause. By the 1890s overcultivation of rice in south Louisiana meant the crop needed more water than the local natural bayous could supply, which led to the development of canal and pump companies. For example, Paul Daniels, the businessman who became suspicious over the sale of Ward Earll's mules, operated the Paul Daniels Canal, pumping water from deep wells to irrigate fields. He and other entrepreneurs typically supplied seed and water for the rice farmers and in return took one-fourth of the crop or proceeds from the sale.[19]

But tensions remained as rice growers and cattle grazers competed for the same rich land. As newsman Dobson pointed out in his 1903 book, "In spring time when grass was not high enough for good grazing, but the field, covered with green, sweet, and tender rice plants, presented temptations to hungry cattle roaming the prairies in search of food, the Earlls would frequently on awakening discover that these animals had breakfasted on the crop they had labored to produce. Ranchmen frequently found their cattle bleeding from gunshot wounds and upon investigation it would be sometimes discovered that the tongues of others had been amputated."[20]

Dobson notes that "ill feeling between the 'yankees' and 'cagens' grew," but by the time the Earlls bought the land they were farming at the time of their deaths, "the rights of 'yankee farmers' . . . had become recognized and the 'natural privileges' of 'cagen' ranchmen more circumscribed . . . [so that] friction between them was less frequent."[21]

At the time of their deaths the Earlls were described as "honest, straightforward, hard-working people" who generally kept to themselves. "By thrift and economy, they . . . were just at the point where they could enjoy the fruits of their labors when the assassin's hand came down with cruel deliberation and remorselessness and cut short their span of life."[22]

5

Welsh

Lemuell Sheldon Earll and his wife, Mary, left Iowa, with their family of small children and moved to southwest Louisiana after 1885. The federal census shows them in Iowa in 1885; land records show that L. S. Earll purchased a right-of-way near Welsh on July 15, 1895, and a larger parcel of land on February 12, 1900.[1] It is possible that the right-of-way was to rented land the Earlls farmed before acquiring their own property.

On arriving in Welsh, the family found a flourishing little town of three hundred people that held the promise of quick growth and a good living to be made.[2]

Like hundreds of their neighbors in Iowa, they had come to southwest Louisiana fleeing a drought that had burned the wheat crop, bitter winter cold that did nothing for their spirits, and the promise of a land of milk and honey by the Louisiana land promoters. The eldest Earll son, Fred, came with the family and stayed in Louisiana until at least 1901 but then apparently went back to Eagle Grove to live with his uncle.[3]

The Earlls came to farm rice in what had been promised to be a land of sunshine and flowers. According to one account, the family couldn't make it by farming at first and moved into the town of Welsh to open a store, but that seems unlikely. More reliable accounts indicate that L. S. and Mary Earll stayed on the farm, which is more reasonable since their entire background was in farming.[4]

The prospects in and around the town were getting better by the day. The farming community twenty-three miles east of Lake Charles via the Southern Pacific line was nestled close to Bayou Lacassine, which flowed to the Gulf of Mexico and sat at the border of the sprawling prairie to the east and magnificent stands of virgin longleaf pine to the north and west.

It was a pretty place, which may have been what attracted the first settler, Miles Welsh, when he decided in the middle 1800s that harsh Pennsylvania winters and his rheumatism could no longer mix and decided to go to Texas looking for a more amenable climate and a place to raise cattle.[5]

He went first to New Orleans and from there began an overland trek that took him across the prairies of southwest Louisiana. About midway through his journey he and his family stopped to set up camp near the Old Spanish Trail, the century-old road that wound through southern Louisiana on its way from Mexico City to Pensacola, Florida.[6]

He'd planned only to rest a spell, but he never left. Instead, he built a home of logs and mud, claimed homesteading rights, and began to provide room and board to cowboys and mail carriers and travelers who were heading to or from the hinterlands and New Orleans. While his wife and daughters took care of the boarders, Miles and his sons began to farm the land.[7]

Miles's oldest son, Henry, left the area for a while to work as an overseer on a plantation in Lafayette Parish, about fifty miles east of Welsh, then joined the Confederate army during the Civil War. But after the war, he and his wife, Sarah Jane Simmons, bought land next to his father's farm and moved their family of four children back to the old home place. Miles died shortly after the war in 1868.[8]

Henry continued to farm until 1880, when the Southern Pacific pushed across the prairie, linking New Orleans to Texas and points west. Henry offered a free right-of-way through his land and provided for a section house under the condition that all trains that passed through had to stop there.[9]

At the same time, Henry had surveyor George O. Elms lay out the beginnings of a town next to the tracks, where Henry built the town's first store. It was operated by his son C. D. Welsh, who was also the first postmaster. Henry brought in a man named Mr. Root to teach C. D. how to run the store. Henry built a house for Root, and C. D. moved into the home when Root moved out.[10]

The railroad opened the prairie to the world, and in April 1887, according to regional historian William Henry Perrin, "the Messrs. Jasinsky and Reever of Guthrie County, Iowa, and George D. Moore, Mitchelville, of same state, visited Welsh and, being captivated with its splendid location and superior surroundings, purchased lands in and near the town."[11]

In July of that year, the entrepreneurs helped to create "a veritable boom in the construction of several good business houses and residences," according to Perrin's account. "About two hundred families of Western and Northern people . . . settled in and around Welsh," and in 1891 the town boasted a two-story school; the *Welsh Crescent* newspaper edited by H. Duggett; "three good hotels, six general stores, one restaurant, livery stable, lumber yard, drug store, market, barber shop, two physicians, and two real estate agents."[12]

In 1891 the railroad hauled out of Welsh some 13,000 barrels of rice and more than 1,500 head of cattle, along with lesser amounts of wool, hay, sugarcane, Irish potatoes, sweet potatoes, oats, and corn.[13] By the turn of the century, Welsh and other farming communities on the prairie were growing at a regular rate, but in 1901 the population began to explode after drillers uncovered the first major oil field in south Louisiana just east of Welsh.

The 1900 census counted a population of 320 in Welsh; the 1910 census recorded four times that many, 1,250.[14] Welsh was a growing, bustling little town, and in the last decade of the 1800s and the first decade of the 1900s, the promise of prosperity attracted farmers and field hands, oilmen and roughnecks, investors and drifters, all of whom saw south Louisiana as a place where quick money could be made.

But in the last days of February 1902 the busy little community was sent into shock by the events on the Earll farm just outside town. "Business has been entirely suspended," the *New-York Tribune* reported. "The murder of the six members of the Earll family has cast an influence over the entire community which makes attention to the ordinary affairs of life impossible."[15]

6

The Arrest

It was only by chance that Ed Batson went to Welsh in the first place and also that he was arrested in Missouri just one day after the discovery of the Earll murders. Like much else in the story of his capture, trial, and eventual death, coincidence played a large role, both in bringing him to Louisiana and his being so quickly apprehended.

Over the course of his legal battles, newspapers offered varying accounts of the accused man's life, but most agreed that his mother, who was divorced from John Batson, and her two sons and a daughter moved when Ed was a small boy to Princeton, Missouri, where his mother ran a lunchroom and boardinghouse, and where he received what the press described as a makeshift education.[1]

According to sometimes unreliable press accounts, Batson's mother married widower Flavius Josephus Payne less than a year before the Earll murders and went to live in Spickard, twelve miles south of Princeton.[2]

"Judging from the best information that could be received," the *New Orleans Picayune* reported, "Ed Batson spent his early manhood working on the sections of the Rock Island road and gradually drifted into the habit of taking long journeys using freight, trains. . . . He came down to Louisiana and tramped into Welsh, where he secured work on Mr. Daniels' rice plantation as a field hand. . . . When Ward Earl purchased his place a few miles west of Welsh, Earl employed him as a field hand."[3]

Ed Batson worked for the Earlls during the rice harvest in the summer of 1901 and was still working for Ward Earll on February 12, 1902. He claimed at the time of his arrest he was

Calcasieu Parish sheriff John Addison Perkins, *seated center*, and some of his associates. This photo was apparently taken some years after the Batson case. *Photo courtesy of the Archives, Frazar Memorial Library, McNeese State University, Lake Charles, LA.*

fired by Ward, who was in a bad mood after staying too long at a Mardi Gras party the night before. The accused man first told his story when he was arrested on February 25 at his sister's home in Princeton, and he never wavered from it until the day of his death.[4]

There are two versions of how Ed Batson was traced to Princeton. In the first version, reported in the *Picayune*, in an amazing coincidence, Sheriff John Perkins of Calcasieu Parish happened to be in New Orleans when he received word of the killings and also just happened to be with a man, identified as a Dr. Williams, who said he knew Ed Batson and also knew that Batson's mother lived in Spickard.

According to the *Picayune*, "Sheriff Perkins . . . received a telegram telling of the murder from his chief deputy. . . . He opened the telegram in the presence of several persons, and naturally uttered an exclamation. Then he read the telegram out loud. One of the friends [later identified as Williams] remarked on the strangeness of things, for he had known where Batson lived, and knew the name of his mother."[5]

The second and more likely version is that part of a letter written to Ed Batson by his mother was found in the gray vest that was left by the scarred mule trader in the buggy driven to the Downs stable in Lake Charles. That caused Sheriff Perkins to send a telegram to Perry Schooler, mayor of Spickard, saying he thought Batson might be headed for Missouri.[6] Sheriff Perkins also had his chief deputy, Charles M. Richard, wire Sheriff John T. Cook of Mercer County, Missouri, describing Batson and the gruesome details of the murder.

Ed Batson had in fact traveled to Missouri during the days after the murder, and he and his brother, Noah, were promptly arrested there. Noah was released when the Mercer County sheriff found that Louisiana authorities had no interest in him, but they held Ed Batson based on an arrest warrant sent by Sheriff Perkins.[7]

The letter accompanying the warrant asked Missouri officials to hold Batson "by all means," because "he committed one of the worst crimes ever committed in the South, or any other country. He killed a man, his wife and four children, shot them with a shotgun and then slit their throats."[8]

Batson had a watch that seemed to be of significance to the sheriff for reasons that never became entirely clear. "Keep his watch safely if he has it on him," Perkins wrote.[9] At one point, prosecutors contended that Batson had taken a watch he stole from Ward Earll to a Lake Charles jeweler to be repaired. The sheriff may have thought Batson was carrying that watch.

Until the day he died Ed Batson claimed that the first he knew of the murders was when he was arrested by Sheriff Cook in Mercer County, and from the day of his arrest, it appears that nobody believed him. "I am not a murderer," he told Sheriff Cook. "I never killed anyone; I am not afraid to go back to Louisiana and tell anything I know about the Earle family, if I am not lynched."[10] He said he had never tried to sell mules or any other livestock in Lake Charles and that in fact nobody there could possibly identify him because he'd never been in the town in his life.[11]

The headline in one of the Lake Charles papers suggested disbelief in that story. "Swift Justice for Ed Batson," it read,

"Despicable Wretch Arrested Last Evening."[12] However, Batson's hometown newspaper was a bit more charitable: "The prisoner was interviewed," the *Princeton (MO) Telegraph* reported, "[and] told a very plausible and well connected story. . . . The circumstances have woven a close net about Batson, and yet his straightforward story, his admission of working for the Earles, of writing the letter found in the vest pocket and his apparent confidence in his ability to account for his whereabouts from the 12th of February to the time of his arrest, has put us to guessing."[13]

Batson always claimed he last saw L. S. Earll and his family several days before he left Welsh and that the entire family was alive and well. He claimed to have gotten along well with the patriarch, L. S. Earll.[14]

However, in an editor's note affixed to the story in the *Lake Charles Weekly American* that reported Batson's account, the editor apparently reflected the view of the citizenry when he basically said that no matter what Batson said, he was guilty. "The above dispatch shows that Batson is already preparing a defense. . . . His story is manifestly false on its face," the editor wrote.[15]

Nonetheless, Batson continued to claim that he worked with Ward Earll up to the day after Mardi Gras, which was on February 11 in 1902, and that on Mardi Gras night Earll went to a neighborhood ball and did not return until early in the morning, "very much under the influence of liquor."[16]

"Ward had been out all night," Batson said. "He said when he started he was going to a dance, and I suppose he did. He had been drinking and was not in a very good humor. I started to clean the stable out and harness the mules, just as I did every day, as my work was driving a team of mules. Gin, one of the bay mules, acted the fool and plunged forward and I jerked her. Ward said, 'That won't do. I guess I don't need you anymore.' Then he paid me $11.25 that was coming to me and I left."[17]

Again, he never wavered from this account through all his trials and interviews. Batson said he "tramped across the fields" to Welsh and got there about ten o'clock in the morning on February 12. He said he had a glass of beer in a saloon in Welsh, talking to the bartender there, before going to the Southern Pacific pump house next to the railroad tracks.[18]

A little after noon he met some men who had been unloading wagons at Paul Daniels's rice mill in Welsh. He said he did not know the last name of one of the men who was named Henry but that the others were Jack Dale, Johnny Henderson, a man he called Smith, and Jim Temple. He talked with them "quite a while" before going back uptown to a saloon for another drink.[19]

Not one of the men named by Batson appears in census records or Welsh directories of the time, but if they were transient workers like Batson, their names most likely would not show up. None of the people he named was called to testify in his behalf.

Batson said the saloon proprietor, thirty-five-year-old William McAffery, who was known as "Mack," was in the saloon when he had his second drink but that he only talked to the bartender. Finishing his drink, he went to the railroad depot and asked when he could get a through freight for Texas. He was told that the next one would not be until one o'clock in the morning, so he went outside to wait at the depot, talking until nearly sundown to two men who were on their way to New Orleans. He then went to a restaurant "next to Paul Daniels place" and bought supper. After supper he went back to Mack's where he saw a number of men, but did not recognize any of them. That night he went to sleep under a boxcar on a side track at Welsh until he caught a passing train about midnight.[20]

"I found it was going to Beaumont, Texas, where I wanted to go," he told authorities, so he got into an empty freight car and rode it to "a little town between Lake Charles . . . and Orange, Texas." He could not remember the name of the town, he said, but thought it was "the last station in Louisiana and the first water tank beyond Lake Charles."[21] The last station in Louisiana was at the town of Vinton, near the Texas border.

He said he got to this little town about daylight on Thursday, February 13, and was there most of the day, the same day when authorities said he was committing murders miles away in Welsh.[22] "There is a little saw mill down there and I went into the barber shop and talked with the proprietor and customers, bought some crackers and cheese in a grocery store for my breakfast," he said. "I stayed in the grocery, waiting for the train west, until noon. Then I went back to the barbershop and went over to the station while the [barber] went to dinner."[23]

That afternoon, he said, he caught another freight for Beaumont, Texas, getting there about sundown, and he "stayed all night down by the oil fields."[24] At that time, Beaumont was one of the hottest places in the fledgling oil industry after discovery of the major Spindletop Field in 1901, and it was a good place to look for work. The Lucas Gusher, drilled by pioneer oilman Anthony J. Lucas, produced more than three million gallons of oil a day, setting off a rush to drill for oil that rivaled the Gold Rush in California. The population of the nearby town of Beaumont went from eight thousand to sixty thousand within a year.[25]

Batson said he went to the pump station next to the Lucas well looking for a place to spend the night but was told that there was no lodging to be had. That night, he said, "I went to the Texas & New Orleans [Railroad] track, built a fire and slept beside it." On Friday, February 14, the day he was alleged to be trying to sell mules in Lake Charles, he said he was still in Beaumont, leaving there on Saturday, February 15.[26]

Batson said he had breakfast at "the first restaurant east of the Lucas well," where he told the proprietor that he [the proprietor] made the best hotcakes in the South. Then, he washed his hands and face and combed his hair at the restaurant and talked to the restaurant man about work and the cost of living. "He told me he could give me $5 a week. He said work was plentiful, but that it would be difficult to get a place to sleep. . . . On the next day I caught a train and went home," Batson said.[27]

From Beaumont, he said he traveled to Missouri in short hitches riding in empty boxcars. Batson said he reached Shreveport on the evening of Sunday, September 16; traveled next on the "No. 30" train into Arkansas; and went from there to Stillwell, which was then Indian Territory but is now in Oklahoma, arriving on Wednesday, February 19.[28]

He said he then went to Pittsburgh in Hickory County, Missouri, and from there to Kansas City, arriving on the evening of Thursday, February 20. According to his account, he spent that night in the Pittsburgh & Gulf roundhouse, where he "put up a good talk with the night watchman and got to sleep by a fire."[29] It was cold that night and snowing, Batson said, and he induced the watchman to let him sleep inside. He said the watchman wanted to know if he was a tramp and let him in only after Batson gave assurances that he was not.[30]

On the next morning, he said, "I got breakfast at Bell's restaurant. Then I walked over the bridge and caught a Hannibal & St. Joe train to Kearney in Clay County. I stayed there until nine o'clock on Friday night, when I caught another train to Cameron, Clinton County." After that he caught Rock Island freight No. 94 and rode it to Altamont in Daviness County.[31]

"I got out of the box car there, ate a sandwich and drank a cup of coffee, then I got into the box car again and went into Trenton," he said, getting there about three o'clock in the morning on Saturday, February 22, which he remembered because it was Washington's birthday.[32]

He stayed around the railroad depot until daybreak, he said, "then went to the boarding house where my brother, J. Noah Batson, lived. We went around together until two o'clock, when we took a passenger train for Spickard. . . . There we met my stepfather's son, John Payne, and he went with us to my mother's and stepfather's home, about five miles southeast of Spickard. We stayed there until Tuesday, the 25th."[33]

He said that day they decided to go to Princeton to see his sister. "We got off the train, went to her house and talked a few minutes, and then I started uptown with my brother to the post office, bought a couple of cigars, and walked back, to my sister's," he said. "In front of the house, Sheriff Cook came along and said he would lock me up."[34]

Batson hinted that the murders may have somehow been because of a dispute within the Earll family itself. "I was tired of working for that outfit," he said. "They were always scrapping, but I want to say that the old man was a pretty decent sort of fellow. On the day I left, the oldest boy was drunk and had been quarreling with his father. The old man said that he was tired of being abused by his sons, and it should be stopped. He did not say what he would do to stop it, but he did say it would be stopped."[35]

Officials in Louisiana and Missouri were more than curious about the box the stranger had given to the Wells Fargo driver that was sent from Lake Charles on February 14 to Batson's mother, Mrs. Payne. They thought it contained valuable evidence, and, according to one news account, was perhaps "a box of valuables stolen from Ward Earll." Mrs. Payne and Missouri authorities went together to the express office to retrieve and open the box. To their astonishment, it contained nothing but rice.[36]

7

Trial by Newspaper

As he was being returned to Louisiana for trial, Ed Batson told a reporter on the train, "I am not guilty. I can prove an alibi." Even Calcasieu Parish sheriff Perkins admitted that the case against him was still wholly circumstantial, observing, "The boy does not look like a murderer, yet all the circumstances point to him."[1]

Still, even before the young man was brought to Lake Charles for trial, it was clear that public sentiment was heavily against him. There seemed to be no doubt in the public mind that he was the killer. Well before his arraignment, a *New Orleans Picayune* headline referred to him as "Batson, the Butcher."[2] In southwest Louisiana, the *Crowley Signal* reported definitively, "The guilt of this horrible crime has been fastened on Ed Batson."[3]

A correspondent for the New Orleans paper who went with Sheriff Perkins to Missouri reported that officials seemed to worry the accused man might be lynched by angry citizens and hinted that a large number of people in southwest Louisiana thought it a good idea to spare the state the cost of a trial.[4]

The *New Orleans Picayune* reported from Welsh,

> The people were so excited that for a time no thought was given the murderer. No such crime had ever before disturbed the erstwhile quiet of this community and the citizens were aghast to think that a human being could perpetrate so foul a deed. . . . But when the first horror of the thing wore off they began to think about the murderer. . . . If he is found and returned here

> there is no telling what his fate will be. . . . It is easy to see [the citizens of Welsh] are not going to allow this inhuman crime to go unavenged.[5]

On February 28, the day Sheriff Perkins reached Spickard to take the accused man into custody, the *Picayune* reported, "[Calcasieu] parish still remains quiet, and while the people are very angry, it is not thought they will resort to violence. The grand jury has been promptly called together and a speedy trial will be urged, with a hope of having the law observed, and the execution of Batson, if found guilty, under the supervision of parish officials."[6] Presumably, that would be preferred over an unsupervised lynching.

The *Picayune* writer stated, "Now that the murdered family [is] buried, and . . . the people are free to stop and consider the whole situation, it seems that indignation waxes stronger and stronger [in Welsh]. . . . [and] cries of revenge come from almost all of the neighboring villages."[7]

Even Louisiana governor William Heard was worried, telling the New Orleans press, "We must protect Batson. The law must be upheld." Heard said he'd given his word to Missouri governor Alexander M. Dockery that "the prisoner will be properly guarded after reaching . . . Louisiana."[8]

Batson and his family had less than sterling reputations in Missouri, the *Picayune* correspondent wrote. "The entire Batson family has the reputation of being hard. Fred [*sic*] Batson, a brother of the prisoner, is a laborer on a narrow-gauge road running out of Princeton, and a sister lives in town with her German husband. . . . Ed Batson, while considered a bad character by the police of Princeton, has only been arrested on small charges."[9] Ed Batson had no brother named Fred. His only brother was Noah.

Authorities in Spickard told newsmen that Batson and his mother had come to the area about five years earlier when his brother-in-law took charge of the electric plant there. According to census data, Batson's mother, her two boys, and her married daughter, Cora, and Cora's husband and children were in Princeton in 1900. Batson's mother, Rachel, and brothers,

Noah and Ed, are all listed as living in the same home on Main Street in Princeton. Ed's sister, Cora Vredenburg, her husband, Adolbert, and their children lived next door.[10]

The sheriff said Batson worked at the plant "off and on" over the next three years, during which time he was arrested once for drunkenness and once for disturbing the peace. While that was made to sound like two separate incidents, it was a single event; he was drunk and arrested for creating a disturbance.[11]

Batson apparently kept his own counsel while being held in Spickard, although he became more loquacious on his way back to Louisiana. According to the *New Orleans Picayune* correspondent, "All the time Batson was lodged in jail in Princeton, Mo. . . . he was constantly under the watchful eye of his extremely shrewd mother and her shrewd husband, and silence was recommended."[12]

During the journey back to Louisiana, Batson at first seemed not to be worried. The *Picayune* correspondent wired from Shreveport that "there was not a lighter hearted passenger aboard the train. Batson led the smoking car in his jokes and told stories of his life at Welsh and told how he had beat his way to Kansas City on a series of freight trains from Beaumont."[13] But, according to the *Picayune*, "He was not in the city of Shreveport five minutes before a train hand identified him as a passenger on a through passenger [train] from Beaumont to Kansas City."[14]

The correspondent reported, "Flagman Turner, who has been running up and down the Kansas City Southern for years, and is a man of his word, stopped directly in front of Batson. He turned to ask Sheriff Perkins if the prisoner was Batson, and when informed, remarked that Batson had been a passenger on the train which left Beaumont about two weeks before."[15] That apparently placed Batson in Beaumont roughly at the time the accused man said he was there, although it put him aboard a passenger train rather than the freights that Batson said he rode. But it seems not to have occurred to the reporter, or anyone else, to ask why the flagman had to ask if the prisoner was Batson before claiming to recognize him. However, had he been called to testify at Batson's trial, Turner's testimony would tend to have corroborated Batson's story that he was long gone from Welsh at the time of the murders. Turner was not called as a witness.

The flagman said he "remembered when Batson boarded his train and took up a seat in the smoker. He was not dressed in the new suit of clothes he is now wearing, but the telltale burn on his cheek was sufficient evidence to confirm this identification at any time."[16]

The famous scar apparently made a lesser impression on a medical man from Shreveport who was "quite a friend of Sheriff Perkins."[17] Identified by the *Picayune* only as "Dr. Williams . . . a member of the Texas Rangers and a man thoroughly acquainted with detective work," he said, "he did not quite remember the man," but that "he had been in the neighborhood of John Downers' [*sic*] stable in Lake Charles when Batson drove in with . . . four mules and six horses and that he recalled the incident of the mules most clearly."[18] However, his clear recollection does not dovetail with that of Lake Charles horse trader John Downs, who spoke of four mules but only two horses.

This appears to be the same Dr. Williams whom Sheriff Perkins was reportedly with in New Orleans when Batson's name was first brought up and who said he knew Batson was from Missouri. It is remarkable that he was in New Orleans just at the right time to speak to the sheriff, was also in the neighborhood of Downs's stable in Lake Charles when Batson allegedly brought in the stock to sell, and then—by accident or design—happened to be on the same train to identify him. With his multiple roles in Batson's capture and identification, it would seem that Dr. Williams would also have been a key witness. However, there is no record of his appearance in either of Batson's trials.

Also, according to the *Picayune* correspondent, a news agent who sold newspapers and magazines to passengers "in passing through the car this morning, stopped and asked if the prisoner was the famous Batson, and when so informed, remarked to Sheriff Perkins that Batson had been a passenger on a train leaving about the time the murder is supposed to have been committed."[19] The news agent said he remembered Batson was on the train headed north about the middle of February. The agent said he not only remembered the scar but he also recalled the fact that Batson "purchased considerable popcorn," a food Batson was said to particularly like.[20]

But the news agent also had to ask if the prisoner was Batson. Neither witness seemed to recognize Batson without first asking who he was. Like Turner, the flagman, the news agent was never called to testify at trial.

About the time those identifications were made, Batson's lighthearted banter disappeared completely, possibly because of fear for his life. From the first he'd recognized there was a danger that he might be lynched, and that danger became even more real once he crossed the state line into Louisiana.

"Formerly he was apparently light-hearted and jolly; now he is quite watchful and nervous. He seems afraid to be in Louisiana," the *Picayune* reported. "From the moment that he crossed the state line he expressed a desire to be in the prison at New Orleans. Walking up the streets of Shreveport, he frequently showed that he had begun to realize he was nearing the end of his journey."[21]

8

Lynching Fears

Sheriff Perkins agreed with his prisoner that there was a real threat that Ed Batson could be lynched by an angry mob, and he took precautions as the train approached the rail yards at the central Louisiana town of Alexandria. He feared "that the people of Welsh and Lake Charles would try to intercept Batson" and that "at that point the yard is dark and filled with freight trains and box cars on the siding. It is counted an ideal place for a lynching party, and some have occurred there," according to the *New Orleans Picayune*.[1]

Just before reaching the rail yard, the sheriff removed Batson's handcuffs and then left the smoking car with his deputies, placing the ever-present Dr. Williams in charge. Batson pretended to be asleep. "There was no evidence that the sleeping passenger was a prisoner, and Sheriff Perkins hoped to throw the lynchers off the track by being found away from the prisoner," the *Picayune* reported.[2]

Fortunately, the precautions were unnecessary. After several anxious minutes in the spooky yard, the train pulled out with no threat of violence. But "Batson, during those few minutes, was thoroughly frightened. He fully expected to be mobbed, and while this expectation lasted, all his old nerve seemed completely vanished."[3]

In view of all this, a nervous Governor Heard ordered Sheriff Perkins to take his prisoner to New Orleans instead of Lake Charles. "I do not believe there would be a lynching in Calcasieu parish," the governor said, "but . . . I will ascertain the true feeling out there."[4]

William Wright Heard (1856–1926) was governor of Louisiana from 1900 to 1904. *Photo courtesy of LOUISiana Digital Library*, http://louisdl.louislibraries.org/.

Despite the fears, the press reported on March 5 that Batson had "crossed the length of Louisiana in safety" and was being held in the parish prison in New Orleans.[5]

Sheriff Perkins and deputy Isaac Fontenot, who went with the sheriff to Missouri to fetch Batson, were "watchful all the way down and were worn out by loss of sleep," but "the cool-headed prisoner showed but little signs of fatigue," taking the trip from his home "very much as he would have a pleasure trip."[6]

Upon reaching New Orleans, "a few kodak [*sic*] fiends" were on hand to take photographs of the prisoner, and "scores of curious persons were met at every point," but Batson was taken to the jail without incident. Then "a *Picayune* man" brought Batson and the authorities who were with him across Canal Street to have his picture taken.[7] Batson insisted that the scar on his face, which he claimed was from a burn when he was a child, be left out of the picture.

"This scar extends from the temple to the corner of the mouth, and seems to have been the result of Batson's coming

Ed Batson did not want his scar to show when this photo was taken for the *New Orleans Picayune*, "Batson in Prison Here," March 6, 1902, 1, 9.

in contact with a rather large piece of hot iron," the *Picayune* reported. "The fact that he wanted the scar hidden attracted the suspicion of the authorities, but, as usual, the prisoner denied completely any criminal connection with the wound."[8]

Despite Batson's insistence, the scar showed up in the photo "through an oversight," and, as reported in the *Picayune*, "it was this scar, which has furnished the tell-tale evidence which is expected to convict Batson for the most horrible crime ever recorded in Louisiana."[9]

After Batson had been photographed, the authorities took him back to the Orleans Parish prison where he was asked to provide a sample of his handwriting, apparently for comparison with the note that was left on the door of Ward Earll's house.[10] He refused, saying an attorney told him to say nothing and write nothing, but jail officials who kept track of Batson's visitors said that he had not yet seen a lawyer.[11] The newspaper's reporter speculated that Batson "had been associating with some of the hardest criminals in the [jail] yard,

This image of the New Orleans jail was made about 1900. *Image courtesy of LOUISiana Digital Library*, http://louisdl.louislibraries.org/.

and had evidently listened to their advice" to say nothing, but the deputies who were watching him in New Orleans wondered about that possibility and about the man himself.[12]

"These men know criminals well," the *Picayune* reported, "and know their many characteristics. They have watched Batson closely ever since he has been in the prison, and they have come to the conclusion that he is a mystery. They realize that the circumstances point strongly to the man's guilt, but it seems wonderful even to these men that a criminal would commit such a wholesale slaughter and then show absolutely no exterior effects of the crime. There is not a man in jail, even those committed for petty offenses to serve a few days' confinement who are more light-hearted and free of anxiety than Batson."[13]

His refusal to give a sample signature may have worked against him. Weeks later, when Batson and his mother finally saw a copy of the note left at Ward Earll's house, Batson pointed out to her that perhaps he should have given the writing sample, because he did not form the letter *B* the same way it appeared on the handwritten note.[14]

"He will stay in New Orleans until the trial is called," the press reported. "Gov. Heard is exerting himself to give the prisoner adequate protection. Batson still protests his innocence."[15]

The plan was to keep the accused man jailed in New Orleans until after a grand jury met in Lake Charles to weigh the charges against him. If the grand jury indicted him, according to the press, "he will be brought [to Lake Charles] for arraignment within a week, so that his trial may take place at once. If the grand jury should fail to indict, which is looked upon as hardly possible, he will be immediately turned loose at New Orleans."[16]

The *Picayune* reporter wrote that in prison, "Batson soon realized that he was [being held] under a serious charge, and would be treated as an exceptionally dangerous man. He is a dangerously cool headed man and one whom no authority can give the slightest opportunity to escape."[17]

However dangerous he might have been perceived to be, Ed Batson continued to claim that he worked with Ward Earll up to the day after Mardi Gras, and that on Mardi Gras night Ward went to a neighborhood ball, got drunk, and fired his hired man the next day because he was hungover and out of sorts.

Meanwhile, in Lake Charles, district judge E. D. Miller called a special session of the grand jury even before Calcasieu Parish authorities returned from Missouri, setting the session for Thursday, March 6.[18] Because of various delays, the grand jury did not take up Batson's case until March 10, at which time Judge Miller "made a brief statement of the frightful crime . . . and urged [the jurors] to make a thorough investigation of the case and to report upon it as speedily as possible."[19]

9

The Dead Tramp

At the very first, when the coroner called together five neighbors of the Earlls to make a preliminary investigation into the gruesome murders, he and the neighbors knew that a tramp had been seen in the vicinity of the crime. They also knew that the town of Welsh was growing quickly and that all sorts of people were riding the freights regularly into southwest Louisiana in search of work. That coroner's inquest concluded nonetheless that Ed Batson alone was responsible for all the murders, that no tramp had anything to do with it.

Calcasieu Parish authorities apparently accepted that decision and never took more than a cursory look at the possibility of another killer. That held true even when the *Washington (DC) Times* ran a story just three days after Ed Batson's arrest under the headline, "Man Who Helped Kill Earls Slain." According to the story, the body of a man named Belsar Dugan, who was also working for the Earlls at the time of the murder, was found near the Earll farm. His throat had been cut in the same way as of some of the Earll family members.[1]

"This fact was known but to few persons, as Dugan was a tramp laborer who had been picked up by the Earls," the *Times* reporter wrote. "He was present at Ward Earl's house during and after the murders and told anyone calling at the house that Earl had gone to Lake Charles. He undoubtedly helped Batson in the murders."[2] The story claimed that Dugan and Batson left the Earll farm together, but only Batson reached Lake Charles. It alleged that Batson killed Dugan in a fight over money stolen from the Earlls. "Unfortunately, the murderers failed to reap the harvest of their crime," the writer said. "One is dead and the other under arrest for seven [*sic*] murders which did not yield enough money to take him out of danger."[3]

There was only one report of the dead tramp found in any of the Louisiana newspapers; his name was not heard again after these stories were published.

The *Abbeville Meridional* reported on March 1, 1902, that on the morning after the Earll victims were found, "the body of Belisan Dugan another victim was found in a thicket."[4] The name of the tramp, if there was a tramp, may actually have been Bélisaire Dugas, a French name that would not have been uncommon in south Louisiana at the time.

No reference to Dugan or anyone else was made in the comments of either the prosecutors or the defense attorneys. Ed Batson was indicted and tried only for the six Earll murders, and the name, or even the presence, of this alleged accomplice never came up during his trials. If there were such a tramp and such a murder, it would seem that others would have written about it in the newspapers. It can be presumed that reporting that the man's throat was cut was intended to link this death to the other deaths and thus to Batson.

But that assertion brings up another missing link in the chain of evidence against Ed Batson: the knife that was supposedly used to cut the victims' throats was not found on the Earll property nor in the wagon left in Lake Charles nor on Batson when he was arrested nor ever.

As we will see, the prosecution went to great lengths during Ed Batson's two trials to describe the heinous wounds and the sheer malevolence of someone who would cut the throat of someone already dead. But no knife or other sharp implement was introduced at either of Batson's trials. The prosecution had no way to place such a knife in the accused man's hands.

Two days before the grand jury took up Ed Batson's case, the *Lake Charles Weekly American* reported that Judge Miller was "anxious to [dispense with] . . . the case promptly, and the people of Welsh will be pleased to see prompt action taken. The delay and the 'goo-goo eyes' Batson seems to be making at the officials and people he comes in contact [with] in New

Orleans is having a rather irritating effect upon [the] Welsh people and all the talk about his good-humor and frank, open conduct in New Orleans makes them weary. They live so near the charnel house on the prairie that they save their sympathy for the butchered Earls."[5]

Authorities speculated that the key to the indictment would be in identifying Batson as the man who had tried to sell Ward Earll's mules in Lake Charles on February 14, and newspaper writers continued a steady stream of reports that they said tied Batson to the animals. The *St. Louis Republic*, for example, reported that Batson had not only been seen in Lake Charles with the Earll stock, but that he had tried to sell Earll animals before.[6]

"Will Martin, who formerly worked with Edward [*sic*] Batson, the alleged murderer of the Earl family . . . says that he was in Lake Charles on February 14 and saw Batson riding in Ward Earl's buggy and leading one of Ward Earl's mules," according to the *Republic* story. "He talked with Batson about the animals . . . [saying] he recognized the mules and a horse as the property of Ward Earl. Batson, he says, denied that Earl owned the animals, saying that they belonged to himself." According to the *Republic*, Martin's statement was so detailed "that the authorities felt in no hurry to send anyone to New Orleans to identify Batson as the man who had tried to dispose of the Earl mules."[7]

The report from the St. Louis newspaper continued:

> Other incidents are coming to light which seem to indicate that Batson several months ago became possessed of a desire to own the Earl team. Early in December Ward Earl loaned Batson the black horse and buggy to travel over to Lake Charles. Batson arrived in the city during the day and accidentally came across William Cogney. Mr. Cogney remarked that the team was a very likely-looking outfit, and Batson at once replied that Cogney could buy it for $100. Then Batson devoted several hours to driving Cogney around town, urging the purchase of the team all the time. Cogney did not care to do business, however, and Batson returned to Welsh.

> On Christmas Day, Batson entered Sam DeShea's stable at Welsh and, calling DeShea to one side, said that he had just received a telephone message from Ward Earl. He had been arrested in Lake Charles and wanted some money. Batson represented himself to be a partner of Earl's and said he would leave the black horse as security for a loan of $10. DeShea refused to advance the money.[8]

As damning as the testimony of these men would have been, however, none of them were called to testify at either of Ed Batson's trials.

On March 8 the *New Orleans Picayune* reported, "The most interesting bit of evidence that has yet come to light on the Batson case was found today. Mr. [A. J.] Findlay, who keeps the hotel at Iowa [Louisiana, about fifteen miles east of Lake Charles], is said to be positively able to identify Batson as a man who stopped at his hotel the night of February 14, with a team of mules."[9]

The press account was apparently incorrect in two instances. When the murders went to court, Findlay testified Batson came to his house, not his hotel, and that it was on February 13, not February 14.

The March 8 story continued, "Batson came there and had an unknown negro with him and wanted to stop over night. The hotel was full, so Batson and his companion slept in a barn. The next morning the negro told Mr. Findlay that Batson tossed around and talked in his sleep all night, so that the negro could not sleep. He said Batson would ask over and over again, 'Have you got a gun? Have you got a gun?'"[10]

The *Lake Charles Weekly American* also reported that the horse trader John Downs was "positive" the photograph of Batson published in the *Picayune* was that of the man who had brought the mules to him on February 14. Downs was taken to New Orleans to make a further identification, and according to a newspaper story, "at the first glance recognized Batson and pointed him out."[11]

Downs said he saw Batson standing in the prison yard among a large number of prisoners, looking at some men repairing an electric light in the yard. The *Picayune* reported this conversation:

> "That's the man. The one with the brown suit of clothes on!" [Downs] exclaimed.
>
> "Which one, which one?" asked his companion, a reporter of the *Picayune*.
>
> His companion had never seen Batson, and turning to Captain Dreyfous, who was in charge at that time, he asked:
>
> "Who is that man with the brown suit of clothes on?"
>
> "Which man?" asked the Captain.
>
> "The one with his hands in his pockets," was the answer.
>
> Captain Dreyfous, who thought he was being joked with, answered in a sarcastic voice: "That? Why that's Batson."
>
> Thanking the Captain, who had not heard the first part of the conversation and not knowing why Mr. Downs had come to the prison, the parties left. The identification was complete and unequivocal and that settled Batson's fate.[12]

Another witness, John LeBlanc, who lived about two miles from the Earll place told the *Weekly American* that on February 13, "while working near his house, he saw Batson driving down the road with a team of Earll's horses hitched to Ward Earll's buggy and leading two span of mules behind the buggy." LeBlanc said he "thought this a little singular." This was a bit different from other testimony that the mules were attached to the buggy and that the horses were being led.[13]

Batson defender Charles Dobson later enlarged upon the fact that LeBlanc saw the man he identified as Batson only from a distance, and that in Dobson's view, it was actually a man who looked very much like Batson.[14]

According to the *Weekly American*, at the time LeBlanc saw Batson, the accused man "was then within four miles of Iowa station, where he stayed all night. This evidence is a new link and connects [Batson] that much closer to his awful crime. It will positively fix almost to the hour his leaving the scene of his butchery."[15]

Neither the newspaper nor the prosecutors answered the question why Batson would remain so close to the murder site if he had in fact just murdered six people. It seems more likely that a man who had just killed an entire family would try to get as far away as he could as quickly as he could, rather than spend the night in Iowa, where he had transacted business and where he or the animals with him could be recognized.

Batson remained in the New Orleans jail while the grand jury in Lake Charles pondered whether to formally accuse him of the Earll murders, and keeping him at a distance from Calcasieu Parish apparently allowed things to cool down a bit. The *Picayune* reported on March 8, "The indignation of the people of [Calcasieu] Parish, while just as intense, [has] been held in check, and now those people who were most pronounced in their talk of speedy vengeance . . . expressed a willingness to await the action of the law."[16]

Sheriff Perkins said he had "every confidence that there would be no violence," that "the circumstantial evidence is becoming stronger daily," and that "the links in the chain seem nearly all in hand."[17] Deputies had found what they claimed to be a new piece of evidence—a pair of bloody gloves—although the sheriff admitted they had not been traced directly to Batson and that his deputies "were still working on that."[18]

10

Another Crime

If Ed Batson was lighthearted and carefree in the New Orleans jail, the public's mood in Lake Charles grew even blacker just a week before the grand jury took up his case. To quote the press account of the day, the body of a nine-year-old girl, Iris Kendall, was found with "her tender little throat . . . cut from ear to ear" and her eyes "wide open with the look of unutterable horror. . . . Her disarranged clothing showed too plainly the nature of the attempt, which preceded the murder."[1]

Although her assault and death had nothing to do with Batson or the proceedings against him, the newspaper pointed out that "Lake Charles has of late sipped her fill of horrors."[2]

At the time of her death, Iris lived with her parents and sister in the Sunset Hotel on the corner of Bilbo and Lawrence streets. The hotel was occupied mostly by Southern Pacific Railroad and Wells Fargo Express employees. Iris's father, R. J. Kendall, worked with a Southern Pacific construction crew and was in Crowley, about forty miles east of Lake Charles, on the afternoon his daughter was murdered.[3]

The Kendalls had just rented a four-room house not far from the Sunset Hotel, and on the fateful afternoon Mrs. Kendall decided to take Iris and her six-year-old sister, Eunice, to see the new house. "I didn't have a key but thought my room key from the Sunset Hotel might fit, so we went to the house to see what furnishings we'd need," Mrs. Kendall told deputy sheriff T. S. Hardy. "The key fit and the children were delighted with the house. We looked it over thoroughly and then at noon we headed home, stopping at a grocery to buy lunch fixings. . . . After lunch the little girls begged to go back. Finally, at 2:00 p.m. I let the oldest, Iris, walk back to the house. I thought she'd be perfectly safe since we knew the neighbors, and children in the neighborhood played outside all the time."[4]

When Iris didn't return in about an hour, Mrs. Kendall sent Eunice to the house to tell her sister to come home. Eunice stopped and talked to William Merritt, who ran a saloon on Railroad Avenue, telling him she was going to find her sister at the new house.

"About twenty minutes later," Merritt told the police, "I saw the youngest child come running back down the street crying. When I asked her what was the matter, she said, 'My sister is hurt and I'm going after mama.'" When the mother and child passed his saloon running toward the house, he went with them. Merritt described the "horrible sight" he and Iris's mother found, and the Lake Charles press reported every grisly bit of it.[5]

Several days later, when no arrests had been made, the newspaper's language was reminiscent of that used in the Batson case. South Louisiana historian Nola Mae Ross quotes the press account: "Forty-eight hours more have passed since the murder of little Iris Kendall," the reporter wrote, "and still the inhuman wretch who killed her remains undetected." The crime and its lack of resolution, the newspaper said, "is enough to goad the people of Lake Charles to frenzy."[6]

"Frenzy" may have been a bit too strong, but the citizenry of Lake Charles was even more determined that no murder was going to go unpunished. After the grand jury voted to indict Ed Batson, it was called upon to also make a "rigid investigation" into the little girl's death, but nobody was ever charged with Iris Kendall's murder.[7]

A newspaper report on the day the grand jury was to meet noted, "This is grand jury day. Twelve . . . men of the parish are in locked apartments of the court house, with urgent, serious business facing them. No matter in the parish can be more serious than the decision whether or not a man now in jail in New Orleans shall be found 'probably guilty.' . . . There are other serious matters ahead of the jurymen [including] the case of Iris Kendall's awful murder."[8]

The little girl's murder went unsolved for six years until the spring of 1908, when a man named Ed Forbes, also known as Jim Sanders, made a deathbed confession of the crime. He died at Fort Gibson in the Indian Territory from injuries received in an accident of some sort. On his deathbed he told his wife about the crime, and she told the story to John Fears, a Lake Charles man who lived for a time in the Indian Territory. Forbes said he had overheard Mrs. Kendall making an appointment with the landlord to look at the house. He said the mother, not the child, had been his intended victim.[9]

According to a press account, "Forbes had been roaming around and coming to the house, saw the door was unlocked, entered and waited for his victim, knowing of the appointment, but not thinking of the child coming over. . . . Forbes caught her and committed the crime, and when she threatened to tell on him, and was persistent in her childish and honest way, he saw . . . there was nothing to do but get rid of her and accordingly murdered her. . . . He stated that he was present with the crowd when the murdered child was found."[10]

11

Indictment and Plea

It was no surprise to anyone that the grand jury quickly returned an indictment against Ed Batson, based partially on the story of a secret, never identified witness who said he'd driven to Ward Earll's place on February 13 and was sent away.

According to the *St. Louis Republic*, the "very important witness" said "he stopped his horses in front of the house and started to enter, when he was accosted by Ed Batson and told that the Earls were all in Welsh and would not be back until evening. The witness then left the house, and Batson stood where he was until the man was well away from the scene."[1] The secret witness was never identified, did not testify at either of Ed Batson's trials, and was never heard from again.

Batson was still in jail in New Orleans while the grand jury deliberated, but arrangements were already in place to quickly bring him to the hostile town of Lake Charles to enter his plea of guilty or not guilty.

The courthouse town where he was to face the bar of justice had a population of 6,680 according to the 1900 census. It did not yet have the 10,000 people needed to be identified as as a city, but it was a growing town, and one with some rough edges. The 1900 population showed an increase of 110 percent over that of 1890, making Lake Charles the third most populous town in the state. A sizable middle class of merchants and mechanics had by then become established in the community, and there was a growing upper class that consisted mainly of people who were involved in the lumber industry.[2]

Even today, huge old homes in the so-called garden district of old Lake Charles stand as reminders of the last decades of the 1800s and the early 1900s, when lumber barons made fortunes cutting and milling hundreds of thousands of acres of virgin longleaf pine growing just north of the town. The Calcasieu River, flowing through the piney woods to the north of Lake Charles, was used to raft the timber to mills surrounding the lake. The cut timber was then carried by schooner down the river to the Gulf of Mexico to be sold in Galveston, Texas; Vera Cruz and Matamoros, Mexico; and other ports. But while the genteel owners enjoyed wealth and advantages, the mill workers were a rough-and-ready crowd.[3]

At the time of the Earll murders, Lake Charles historian Maude Reid recalled, "Our town was humming with fifteen big saw mills around the town . . . and we probably had twice that number of saloons. Every corner grocery sold beer and cheap corn liquor. Railroad Avenue was then known as 'Battle Row' for its numerous fights and sudden deaths."[4] In the year of 1900 alone, the Lake Charles town council issued thirty permits for saloons.[5]

Thomas Watson, former head of the history department at McNeese State University in Lake Charles, said in an essay about another crime in the city's rowdy past, "Saloons abounded and some catered to a rough clientele. Barroom brawls were not uncommon."[6]

Because of the excitement in Lake Charles and the potential volatility of anger fueled by alcohol, Sheriff Perkins and the deputies who were bringing Batson to town decided to make an intermediate stop in Lafayette, midway between New Orleans and Lake Charles, and hold Batson there for a night, just for safety's sake.

The *New Orleans Picayune* reported the following from Lake Charles on March 19:

> Interest in the famous Earll murder runs at fever pitch. . . . People crowd the street corners, discussing the approaching arrival of Batson. But among all this mass of humanity there seems no single person who even suggests a possible unlawful act by a mob. There is to be no mob law. . . . These facts are plain here. But Sheriff Perkins did not wish to take the slightest

> chance. . . . He . . . quietly dropped off the train early this morning at the coal chutes at Lafayette, and he, with Deputy Carruthers, hurried Batson through the darkness to the Lafayette Parish prison.[7]

Ed Batson remained in Lafayette until Wednesday, March 19, when the early morning train brought him to Lake Charles for his arraignment. The train stopped briefly on the outskirts of town before its arrival at the regular passenger station to allow Sheriff Perkins to lead his prisoner off the train and to a wagon guarded by two deputies.[8]

"The four men, sheriff, deputies and accused, were driven rapidly into the town," where "the sun had not risen when the turnkey closed the heavy iron door on him," the *Lake Charles Weekly American* reported. "Batson seemed calm. Since the town of Welsh had been passed he had experienced no dread of mob violence. A hearty breakfast was prepared. He ate with satisfaction."[9]

By sunrise, the news that he was in town had spread rapidly through Lake Charles, and by nine o'clock the curious began to fill an open lot between the courthouse and the jail. Deputies "thoroughly armed" were inside the jail and at the entrance. There were no signs of trouble, only curiosity. The courthouse was abuzz with people who wanted to know when the infamous Batson would be taken to court to answer a murder arraignment.[10] The arraignment was set for 2:00 P.M., and the prisoner waited quietly on his cot for his first appearance at the bar of justice.

As he looked around him, Ed Batson surveyed a jail far more primitive than the corrections facilities we think of today. The place that would end up being his home for the rest of his short life was built nearly twenty years earlier, in 1883. It was the second jail erected on the two-plus acres donated by local citizens in the 1850s.

The first jail, built in 1852, was a single-story log building that was "improved" in 1866 with the addition of a second story, also made of logs. The two-story 1883 jail that housed Ed Batson was the first brick building in Lake Charles, and,

This 1938 postcard shows the relationship of the jail (white building, *center*) and the courthouse (brown building, *left*). Batson was held in an earlier jail building at the same site. *Image courtesy of the Archives, Frazar Memorial Library, McNeese State University, Lake Charles, LA.*

according to Maude Reid's history, "Conditions were somewhat better in this new jail, but far from what we would now call humane."[11]

The prisoner had all the morning and early afternoon to take stock of his new surroundings. Shortly before 2:00 P.M. deputies cleared the vacant lot between the jail and the courthouse of onlookers and escorted Ed Batson from his stark cell to his arraignment hearing.

Those who could see what was happening saw "a tall, broad-shouldered, stooping young man of strong build and brown healthy face . . . handcuffed heavily."[12] Officers were on either side of the prisoner as he crossed the yard between the buildings, and another walked behind him. He smiled and chatted with the deputies during the minute or so it took to enter the courthouse and reach the upstairs courtroom, but by then, the *Lake Charles Weekly American* reported, Ed Batson was "the only man there whose heart seems not to beat with quickening patter."[13] There had been some talk that a

District Attorney Joseph Moore Jr. led the prosecution. *Photo courtesy of the Archives, Frazar Memorial Library, McNeese State University, Lake Charles, LA.*

prominent law firm in New Orleans would represent Batson at the arraignment, but that turned out not to be.

The room was packed with sightseers when court proceedings began at 2:15 P.M., as district attorney Joseph Moore Jr. rose to suggest that the court appoint attorneys to represent the accused man. Judge Miller "cast his eyes about the room looking towards Lawyers Winston Overton and Paul Sompayrac. . . . The attorneys came forward, spoke to Batson [and] after retiring to an anteroom [for] a moment requested that arraignment be deferred until 9 o'clock [the next] morning."[14]

Neither of Batson's appointed attorneys had any extensive background in criminal law. Overton, who was the city attorney, was then thirty-two years old and had received his law degree ten years before in 1892. He later became a district judge and still later was elected to the state supreme court.[15] Sompayrac, who shared a practice with Overton, had also been practicing in Lake Charles for about ten years. After the Batson trial he moved his practice to New Orleans and later became an assistant attorney general for Louisiana.[16]

Defense attorney Winston Overton. *Photo courtesy of the Archives, Frazar Memorial Library, McNeese State University, Lake Charles, LA.*

With attorneys appointed, deputies again handcuffed Batson and escorted him back to jail. The judge ordered everyone to stay in the courtroom for two minutes to let the prisoner and the deputies get across the vacant yard. "The proceedings were all quiet but rather dramatic," the *Weekly American* reported. "Not more than a half hour was taken up."[17]

Proceedings were no less dramatic the next morning when Batson returned to court, appearing young, strong, and "decently clad" as he entered the courtroom accompanied by "the slender sheriff in [a] light suit and his younger deputy . . . [who] un-iron[s] the hands of the captive. [Batson] follows one and goes ahead of the other . . . up through a gate to a seat where all can see him." He watched as the judge seated himself at the bench, surrounded by "the business like clerk" and the lawyers.[18]

The newspaper account continued: "Across the enclosure comes one of the lawyers assigned to defend him. The big prisoner follows the beck of the attorney to the anteroom behind his honor," with a deputy sheriff accompanying them, because "there is a window . . . and the jump is but thirty feet to the ground."[19]

When they returned to the courtroom, Batson's lawyers objected to the arraignment, arguing that the grand jury made a mistake in the way it indicted him. They argued that he had been charged with six murders, but only as a single offense. Under state law, they said, there should be a separate indictment for each of the deaths, a claim they would eventually take to the Louisiana Supreme Court. Judge Miller ruled, however, that the indictment was legally performed and declared it was time for Ed Batson to make his plea.[20]

> The huge-grown young man lumbers over to within a yard of the judge. There is not a sound in the court. He stands erect, rather less composed than [the day before]. Every moment or so he puts up his hand and brushes pettishly the back of his head.
>
> He looks toward the judge until he hears the Clerk, just in front speaking and he turns his attention that way. This is a document needing a minute of quick reading. The clerk is rapid. Yet the last sentence is all that the prisoner needs to hear. He is being told that he, Albert E. Batson is charged by the State of Louisiana with willfully and feloniously murdering Ward Earle and five other members of the Earle family on February 12, 1902. "Are you guilty or not guilty?" asks the clerk of court.[21]

The newspaper account says only that the prisoner gave an answer to the question. We presume that he said, as he had all along, that he was not guilty of the crime.

And that was that. The prisoner was returned to his guarded cell by the lakefront to await his trial, which was set by Judge Miller for April 14.[22]

12

A Mother's View

Ed Batson did have one staunch believer in his innocence. In reading the accounts of the court proceedings and of his eventual death, some of the most moving passages are of the trials, perseverance, and ultimate heartbreak of his mother, Rachel Batson Payne, who was steadfast in her belief that her son simply could not have committed such a brutal crime.

Despite her sometimes unflattering portrayal in the newspapers, it is apparent from press accounts that there was a deep bond of affection and trust between mother and son. When she arrived in Lake Charles for her son's trial, she presented a far different picture of herself and of her son than had so far been portrayed in the press. For the next eighteen months, she agonized over her son's plight and fought for his life, even when everyone else had given up hope.

She was born Rachel "Rae" Stottlemire on February 10, 1858, in West Virginia. She came from a pioneer family that had been in America since before the revolution, and she had already seen her share of troubles. Her parents were John Stottlemire, who was born in 1820 in Virginia and died in 1874 in Grundy County, Missouri, and Priscilla Hexenbaugh, born in Pennsylvania on May 18, 1828.[1]

Her family had been in America since David Stadlemayer, who was born in Munich, came to Maryland sometime before 1760. His son George Stottlemyre (as the name was spelled then), Rachel's great-grandfather, was born in Frederick County, Maryland, in 1759, and George's son, David, apparently was the first to use the spelling Stottlemire. He was born in Frederick County in 1784. David married Mary Curfman,

Rachel Stottlemire Batson Payne. *Photo reproduced by permission from Catherine Todd.*

John Batson. *Photo reproduced by permission from Catherine Todd.*

also of Maryland, and they apparently moved to Virginia before 1820, the year when Rachel's father was born.[2]

Rachel Stottlemire was still a little girl, not yet thirteen years old, when she married John Batson on October 22, 1870. The Batson and Stottlemire families had traveled together from Virginia to Missouri years earlier. It was common for such fellow travelers to set up farms close to each other, attend the same church, and generally socialize together, which commonly led to multiple marriages among families. In fact, Rachel's sister, Susan, married John's brother, James.

In July 1876, nearly six years after John and Rachel's marriage, daughter Cora was born. Two more children followed: James Noah in August 1878, and Albert Edwin "Ed" in April 1881. Rachel and John parted ways when the children were still very young. Rachel subsequently married again several times, including a remarriage to John Batson for another short and unhappy stint.[3]

Rachel and John Batson separated for good when Ed was still very young. Rachel married again after twice divorcing John, but that marriage appeared to be a short-lived affair, and we found no record of it except that she is declared as Mrs. Rachel Foster in the 1900 U.S. Census and listed as divorced. She was briefly married to a man named Chambers and married twice-widowed, sixty-seven-year-old Flavius Josephus Payne of Spickard on July 16, 1901.[4]

Through correspondence with Batson family members we know that Joe Payne was a wealthy man by Missouri standards of the day. By the time he married Rachel, most of his children, except for a teenage daughter, had started their own families. Although Payne apparently did not come to Louisiana himself, his relative affluence allowed Rachel to travel to Lake Charles to show support for her son during the long months of 1902 and 1903 when he was on trial for his life. She came to Lake Charles at least three times, staying for extended periods at the Walker House, a boarding hotel that was located not far from the courthouse.

At the time of her son's arrest, the *Picayune* called Rachel Payne "shrewd," with the inference that she was also shrewish, but she was able to change that impression when she traveled to Lake Charles. She made no bones about it: she thought her son was innocent and would be proven so in court. She had come to the town to support him, and did so actively, creatively, and intelligently, despite the emotional burden it must have placed upon her. The newspapers portrayed her as a woman of bearing and dignity, something borne out by her few surviving photographs. For example, the *Lake Charles Weekly American* reported,

> The lady is not elderly and has a most pleasant disposition. She is a plain, easy conversationalist . . . shows no excitement, and speaks freely.
>
> Those people who picture Mrs. Joseph F. [*sic*] Payne . . . as an old woman with head bowed in tears and face wrinkled from grief would be very much surprised to come in contact with her. . . . [She is a] tall, erect lady with an imposing carriage and a clearly defined and determined countenance with a pure, easy voice—a woman who in the course of speaking looks her auditor square in the eye and exhibits no nervousness.[5]

She said her son had never been in any serious trouble before and that it was "hard for [her] to believe that he is the murderer of the six Earlls, for he was always so tender-hearted and quiet."[6]

In his mother's words, Ed was always a delicate and loving boy. No doubt she still viewed him as a child—he was in his early twenties—as he stood accused of six gruesome murders. In her eyes he was still the kind little boy she had reared, and when she heard the accusations against him, she thought they were ridiculous—her Ed could not do something like that.[7] When first told of the accusation, Ed himself thought someone was playing a cruel joke on him. As for Rachel, it was simply impossible for her to imagine that her boy could do such a thing.

From all accounts, she was an intelligent and hard-working woman who quickly set about the task of helping her accused son. Over the next year and a half she displayed creativity and

Rachel Stottlemire Batson Payne with Alta Eloise, Edith, and Velma Batson, the children of her son James Noah. *Photo reproduced by permission from Catherine Todd.*

Rachel Stottlemire Batson Payne with her sister Nancy Ann Stottlemire. *Photo reproduced by permission from Catherine Todd.*

determination in trying to bring about his exoneration. Lawyers had volunteered to come to Lake Charles from Missouri to defend her son for free, she said, but she refused their offer because she had full confidence in the attorneys appointed by the court in Lake Charles.[8]

According to the press, "She feels that her boy is innocent and knows that he will have a fair trial and there is nothing to hinder her from believing that he will come clear. She has full confidence and trust in the two attorneys of Lake Charles who will defend him. They are shrewd lawyers, she says, and just now know a whole lot and say little—something that makes an excellent showing for them and inspires her with confidence."[9]

Rachel Payne described her son as "a most forgiving boy" who was "very affectionate to his mother and often declared that he wouldn't give [up] his dear mother for all the pretty girls in the world." She said that he was "tender-hearted and would sicken at the sight of blood—traits . . . that cling to him . . . to this very day."[10]

Rachel said Ed found work on the railroad when he finished his schooling but didn't like it very much, and on August 12, 1901, his older brother's birthday, he'd kissed her good-bye and told her he was going to Oklahoma with some other men to work cattle. From there he wandered to the sawmill town of Vivian, in Caddo Parish in northwest Louisiana, and worked there for several months. After that he went to Welsh to work on the Earll farm and help with the rice harvest. He wrote to her regularly to let her know where he was and what he was doing.[11]

Rachel said her son had written to her in early February to tell her he was returning to Missouri. She was not called to testify about this letter that tended to show that Batson was not fleeing from a crime but had planned for some time to return to Missouri, nor was the letter itself introduced in either of his trials.

When he got home, she said, he told her he'd neglected his writing during the rice harvest because he was very busy with the work, and that "Mrs. Earll treated him so well and just like a mother that he did not realize that time had been slipping by so swiftly." He spoke very fondly of the Earll family, saying that all of them had treated him nicely, even Maude Earll, whom he described as "just a little proud and haughty, but nevertheless kind."[12]

The Ed Batson who returned to Missouri was the same Ed who left, she said. There was "no cloud" in his thoughts, and he "did not sneak into Missouri but came openly" so that everyone knew of his arrival. He had only one dollar in his pocket when he came home, and his brother gave him the money for a new suit of clothes.[13]

Despite allegations to the contrary in some news reports, she said her son had wanted to return to Louisiana to clear his name. She believed the facts—or lack of them—would exonerate her son and that he had an alibi that could be supported by witnesses. Unfortunately, none of those witnesses were ever called to testify.

The *Weekly American* reported, "Mrs. Payne contradicted the newspaper talk that her son refused to be brought back to Louisiana without requisition papers. It was false. He was willing to come back and told her he would return to Missouri soon [after he had proved] his innocence without a doubt. The people in Missouri, who know him, believe likewise and as for her she cannot be shaken from her convictions. . . . She knows that Ed is falsely accused and no other person is more eager than she for the murderer of the Earlls to be apprehended and dealt swift justice."[14]

13

Confusion, Confrontation

If John Downs was certain of his identification of Batson in New Orleans, some others in Lake Charles weren't so sure. Men who thought they knew Batson could not pick him out of a line of prisoners.[1]

According to a report in the *Jennings Daily Record*, "Three prominent residents of Calcasieu Parish—two of whom thought they knew him on sight—failed to pick him out when the prisoners were lined up in the parish jail yard."[2]

One of them, Walter Meyer, "stood by the side of the buggy the evening someone tried to sell the span of Earll mules in Lake Charles. He took a good look at the driver and believed that he would know him again."[3] Meyer picked another man from the lineup.

According to the press report, "All the prisoners were lined up, there being about twenty-five in the row. The men were made to hold their heads up and their faces straight ahead, keeping their eyes on a certain post, while the inspection was going on. . . . Walter Meyer walked up to one prisoner, and laying his hand on his shoulder said: 'That looks like the man I saw in the buggy trying to sell the mules.'" The man was not Batson, it was another prisoner named Harry Howard.[4]

William P. Russell Jr., superintendent of a rice mill in Welsh, was next to make his identification. He said he knew Batson because he'd sold feed to him on several occasions. However, Russell identified another prisoner, R. J. Wilson, as the man who bought feed at his mill.[5] However, neither of the men Meyer and Russell picked from the lineup and claimed was Batson had a facial scar.

Family members believe this to be a photo of Fred and Maude Earll. *Photo reproduced by permission from Patty Shealy.*

The third man, former police jury president Adolph Meyer, said he would not know Batson and could not identify him as one of the men in the lineup.[6] It's unclear why he was called to participate in the lineup in the first place.

It is understandable that none of these men appears to have been called as a witness for the prosecution when Batson's trial began. It is not so understandable why they were not called by the defense. But misidentifications or not, Ed Batson was put on trial, and as it began, at least three people were certain he was the murderer.

On the day testimony in Batson's trial was scheduled to begin, Fred and Maude Earll went to the Calcasieu Parish jail for an extraordinary, emotional confrontation with the man they believed to be the murderer of their parents and siblings. "The scene was sad and dramatic and the memory will linger long with those who beheld it," according to the *Grundy County (MO) Gazette*.[7]

Maude, Fred, a woman identified as Fred's wife, and "two or three ladies" went to the jail about 9:00 A.M., according to the newspaper story, and were taken by the sheriff and two deputies to the cell where Batson was confined. Members of the party said Batson "was as white as a ghost, his hands trembling with emotion" as Maude looked him "fixedly" in the face, but that he silently returned her gaze. "The poor girl, whose whole life is darkened by grief, was also much affected," according to the press report. "She attempted to speak, but what she said was inarticulate."[8] Fred, however, had no trouble speaking.

"Batson, this is all you have left me of my family," he said, pointing at Maude.

"Batson seemed struggling for breath as he tried to answer," the writer reported, "but he also could not be understood."[9]

The encounter lasted only a few minutes before one of the ladies accompanying the Earlls broke the "tense and painful silence" and suggested they leave. According to the account, Maude "seemed to be fascinated by the man she believes has wrought such misery upon her."[10]

Given Maude Earll's state of mind and the fact that she once said she was afraid of Ed Batson,[11] one wonders why she would ask for such a meeting or whether she really wanted to be there. Batson appeared agitated for a little while after the visitors left, but his agitation soon passed, and he was quickly "the same careless, joking youngster as before," the reporter continued. "He has a remarkable nature, let him be innocent or guilty."[12]

It is most probable that Fred Earll was the instigator of the jailhouse visit, or perhaps it was the woman who was identified as Fred's wife but who was more likely his aunt; there is no record of Fred being married at that time. The aunt, Mrs. John W. Earll, née Lavantia White, was the sister of Mary White Earll, who was Fred and Maude's mother.[13]

While Fred's aunt's regular appearance in court was reported and Fred is mentioned as being present at this confrontation, his name is strangely missing in other newspaper stories one would think would have mentioned him. He said he was in the state of Iowa when he was notified of his family's deaths on February 25 and "left that very same day" for Louisiana. He had not arrived on February 27 but was "expected on every train" arriving in Lake Charles on that day and the next, according to press reports.[14] But there is no mention of him at the burial of his slain parents and brothers on March 1. Press accounts make much over how the funeral cortege passed in front of the residence where an emotional Maude was staying but make no mention of Fred.[15]

He did arrive in Lake Charles on or before March 8, the day he told reporters he had no intention of selling the Earll farms, part of which he presumably would inherit. He said he would sell some of the stock but keep the land.[16] Saying that he would sell some stock is curious, as other reports indicate there was no stock to be found with the exception of the horses and mules that were brought to Lake Charles.

When Batson first went to trial, the newspapers noted that Maude and her aunt "took seats just in the rear of the state's attorneys," but make no mention of Fred being in the courtroom or even in the courthouse until he was called to testify. When he was called, he testified that he was in the state of Iowa when he was notified of the deaths of his parents and siblings and that he had been away from Welsh "a little over a year." He was not asked and did not volunteer the reason he left Louisiana, but there are some indications that a rivalry between Fred and his younger brother Ward might have had something to do with it.[17]

Fred came to Louisiana with his parents when the Earlls first moved to a farm near Welsh and apparently worked with his siblings on the farm. But even though Fred was the eldest of the brothers, U.S. Census forms of 1900 show that Fred is still just a farmhand on the family farm, while Ward is listed as owner of part of the property.[18] It would seem that the older boy would get the first crack at buying land from the family, circumstances that raise the question of whether he was passed over for some reason or declined the offer of the property himself and left Louisiana.

In denying his guilt, Ed Batson claimed there was bad blood between the brothers, and he once had to intervene in a fight in which gunplay was threatened. The Lake Charles authorities and newspapers apparently did not believe Batson, but there is circumstantial evidence that his account might have been true.[19]

But perhaps the most curious thing is that Fred gave newspaper reporters an almost to-the-penny account of how much money each of the victims was carrying at the time of the crime. If he was hundreds of miles away in Iowa, how did he know that?[20] Nobody asked, and, again, he did not volunteer the information.

14

The Case Is On

Even though the case against him was wholly circumstantial, it was evident from the first day in court that the state would accept nothing less than the death penalty for Ed Batson, a proposition the presiding judge had no problem with. But even others in the press recognized that the local newspapers had already tried and convicted the confident young man from Missouri. On April 19, 1902, the *Houston Daily Post* printed this opinion:

> The famous Batson case is on, and the suspect with the "smooth, happy, boyish face" is being assayed to see if his life is forfeit. The case is of peculiar interest, not only because of the frightful circumstances and extent of the crime, but from the stoicism of the suspected man and the attitude of newspapers in that locality and men who seemingly wish to convict him before a trial is had. There is plenty of time to talk of the man's crime after he is convicted, and if he is the right man there will be an execution in the Lake Charles jail yard. Although Batson has much to explain, and may not explain it, yet it is undeniable that public sentiment has been worked up against him by newspapers, and it will be a harder job because of such to give him a good case.[1]

The presiding judge, Edmund Denis Miller, was known as a law-and-order man. He was an 1888 graduate from Tulane University, who started out as a sugar planter and cattleman and had served as sheriff of Cameron Parish before taking up legal studies.[2]

On April 19, 1902, the *Lake Charles Weekly American* reported, "Just sixty days from that on which L. S. Earll, his wife and four sons perished and forty-nine days from that on which the remains of the slaughtered family were discovered, Albert Edward [*sic*] Batson was placed on trial for his life. . . . Considering all the machinery that had to be put in motion, the inquiry into the bloodiest crime that ever stained the annals of Louisiana has followed close on the heels of its commission."[3]

People came from far and wide to see the beginning of the trial. The *Weekly American* reported: "Ordinarily, Lake Charles people take little interest in court proceedings. . . . There are few idle people in Lake Charles or the parish at any time and usually the attendants at court are limited to those immediately interested in the particular case on trial. But today, even though the preliminaries were as interesting as a patent office report, the room was thronged by people from over the parish and even the aisles partially filled."[4]

Ed Batson's mother entered the courtroom a few minutes before nine o'clock, when the proceedings were scheduled to begin, "taking a seat just behind the space reserved for the accused and his attorneys." She was solemnly attired in black, and her "keen, dark features and tall spare figure made her easily recognizable. . . . Her manner was calm; but her mother's heart betrayed itself in the absorbed interest she showed in even the most trifling preliminaries."[5]

Maude Earll and her aunt, Mrs. J. W. Earll, sat on the opposite side of the aisle, just behind the prosecutors.[6] The only remaining Earll son, Fred, was not mentioned in the accounts of the opening of the trial.

The buzzing of voices in the courtroom turned to silence as Ed Batson "came in quietly in charge of Sheriff Perkins, walked over to where his mother was sitting and kissed her, afterward sitting down by his counsel. . . . [He] looked extremely neat and prepossessing. Not a shadow of fear rested on his smooth, boyish face, and he betrayed no emotion under circumstances that would try any man's nerves, innocent or guilty."[7]

The preliminaries included a motion by Batson's attorneys to throw out his indictment on the grounds that the name of prospective grand juror Thomas Patrick appeared in two places on the list of names drawn to select the panel that indicted Batson. The attorneys argued that the law required 300 different names on the list of prospective jurors, but since Patrick's name was there twice, the list contained only 299 separate names. That, they said, made the grand jury improperly constituted, and thus the indictment it returned was invalid. Prosecutors rebutted that no fraud was intended and no harm done. The judge agreed with the prosecutors, overruled the objection, and all was set for the selection of the men (no women served on Louisiana juries in those days) who would determine Ed Batson's fate.[8]

It took two days to pick a jury. Juror after juror was rejected by the prosecution either after saying he did not believe in capital punishment or that he would not send a man to death based only on circumstantial evidence. Forty-seven potential jurors were examined before twelve could be seated. In each instance, prosecutors asked the prospective juror specific questions about his belief in capital punishment and his view on circumstantial evidence.[9] In Underwood's words, "In the argot of today's trial lawyer, the jury was 'death qualified.'"[10]

When jury selection was finally completed, the following made up the panel of jurors:

- D. D. Savoie, who had moved to Jennings, about fifteen miles from Welsh, twelve years before, told the court he had formed no opinion about Ed Batson's guilt or innocence but that he favored capital punishment and could convict on "very strong" circumstantial evidence.
- Jesse Andrus, also of Jennings, who swore he had no fixed opinion of guilt or innocence. He said, "Being a fair-minded man, I feel that I would be at ease in my own conscience in returning a verdict according to the evidence."
- H. H. Hoag, a thirty-year-old employee of First National Bank in Jennings. He moved to southwest Louisiana from the state of Iowa, as had the Earlls.

- David Marcantel, place of residence not given. He said he could “bring in a verdict of death with an easy conscience.”
- J. A. Grimaldi, who resided in the town of Westlake, located on the northwestern side of Lake Charles. He said he had no scruples against the death penalty and he could convict on circumstantial evidence if it was “very positive.”
- D. W. Oliver, of Westlake. His responses to questions were not recorded by the press.
- E. H. Green, also of Westlake, and also silent in the press accounts.
- Dan Beyer, of Westlake, who said he was unbiased against the prisoner.
- G. W. Elender, of Westlake, who “felt a little uncertain, but could convict on sufficient evidence whether direct or not.”
- D. A. Leveque, of Lake Charles, about whom the record is silent.
- J. Alton Foster, of Lake Charles, whose remarks are also unrecorded.
- Paul Sullivan, “who answered the old familiar questions without delay and was acceptable to both sides.” He became the foreman of the jury.[11]

The state based its case on several key points:

1. The Earlls did not commit suicide or kill each other, since no weapon was found near any of the bodies.
2. Their houses had been searched, presumably for money.
3. Their stock had been stolen and driven to Lake Charles by a man who attempted to sell the animals and then abandoned them.
4. On the same day the stranger attempted to sell the stock, a man had Ward Earll’s watch repaired by a Lake Charles jeweler.
5. On that same day a man giving the name of C. R. Batson left Fay Earll’s shotgun with a Lake Charles gunsmith to be repaired and never came back for it.

6. The buggy abandoned in Lake Charles contained a letter from Batson's mother to her son, another letter signed by Batson that the state claimed was evidence he intended to commit suicide, and a clock that belonged to Ward Earll.
7. The same man who had gone to the jeweler and gunsmith sent an express package that day to Ed Batson's mother in Missouri.
8. Therefore, Batson was the man who was trying to sell Ward Earll's stock and must be the man who committed the murders.[12]

According to the theory put forward by the prosecution, Ward Earll, hungover or sick, was killed in his bed. Fay, who was at the house tending to his sick brother, heard the shot, ran into the room, and was gunned down. The two younger boys, John and Lemmie, were killed when they stopped at Ward's house on their way home from school. Mrs. Earll was killed after she went to the house when the younger boys' ponies showed up at her home without them, and her husband, L. S., was then hunted down in the field, shot, and thrown in the ditch.[13]

"Batson was in his seat early and wore the same imperturbable expression that has characterized him throughout," according to a news account. "Maude Earle came forward with her aunt, Mrs. J. W. Earle, and they took seats just in the rear of the state's attorneys."[14]

The coroner, Dr. Watkins, was the first witness for the prosecution when the court was gaveled to order on Wednesday, April 16, and spent much of the morning providing a graphic description of the grisly scene he found when he was called to Ward Earll's house.[15]

Making a rough drawing, Watkins pointed out where each of the bodies were found and said the room was bloodstained and shotgun pellets were lodged in its west wall. The bed where Ward Earll was found was saturated with blood. Judging from the decomposition of the bodies, the victims had been dead for ten days or two weeks before they were discovered. He testified that Ward had been shot in the eye, destroying the eyeball and fracturing the skull, two of the younger boys had been shot in the face and their throats slit, and another was shot in the back of the neck. The wound on Mrs. Earll's face was burned with gunpowder, indicating she had been shot at close range, and her entire face was blown away.[16] L. S. Earll had been found the next morning, the coroner said. He had been shot in the breast with fine shot, thrown into a ditch, and covered with straw.[17]

On cross-examination by defense attorneys, the coroner said he removed shot from the wounds of the victims, but he could not produce it in court because it had been lost. He also testified that he had made no scientific test to prove that blood found on the floor in Ward Earll's house was human blood. "It was blood but [I] cannot positively say from a human being," he said.[18]

"A good many ladies were present in the courtroom" when deputy sheriff Thomas Hardy took the stand after lunch and continued the gruesome description of the murder scene. He reiterated much of the coroner's testimony and said that a trunk beside the bed in the death room was "all upset" and that he found a collar and a necktie behind the trunk. Ward Earll was clothed but was not wearing a collar, he said. He also found a pair of gloves nearby.[19]

Hardy said he found four tacks on the front door of the cabin and some knife prints on the door near the tacks. He also found five empty twelve-gauge shotgun shells in the house and said the shot in the west wall of the murder room was No. 4 shot. When he was cross-examined, he said he pried some of the shot from the wall, but that he also lost this evidence.[20]

Deputy Isaac Fontenot, who was one of the first lawmen to reach Ward Earll's house, was called to the stand to add detail to the gory scene already described by the other witnesses. Old trousers were tied around the necks of some of the victims whose throats had been cut, he said. Mrs. Earll was clad in a calico dress and had a mackintosh coat around her shoulders. He said the "small boy" (Lemmie) had a hat that was bent over his face and badly stained with blood. He and John wore clothes that they might have worn to school. He identified a glove as the one someone picked up near the body of L. S. Earll.[21]

On cross-examination, Deputy Fontenot said he had lived in Welsh for thirty years and knew the Earlls personally but could not say whether they were generally liked or disliked in the community. He said the Earlls spoke no French, and the nearest neighbors spoke little English, so the Earlls kept pretty much to themselves. He said he did remember an incident that happened about six years earlier in which someone cut barbed wire on the Earlls' property but recalled no details. He also said a number of "tramps, hobos, sports and strangers" passed through Welsh during the winter.[22]

The testimony by the coroner and investigating deputies gave the jury a vivid impression of the terrible scene lawmen found when they were called to Ward Earll's little house, but not a word of it connected Ed Batson to the bloody room where the bodies were found stacked one upon another, nor did it establish when the murders took place. The witnesses identified no murder weapon, no bloodstained knife used on the throats of the dying or already dead victims, and the prosecutors could not even produce the shotgun pellets they claimed killed the victims.

As the testimony stood at the end of the first morning, it was certain that a horrible crime had been committed. But not even a circumstantial link to Ed Batson—or any other person—had been established. That would be the task of the witnesses who were called to the stand when court resumed after lunch—beginning with the gripping account by Maude Earll of her discovery of her murdered mother and siblings.

Ed Batson "looked her fairly in the face," while she testified "with tears in her eyes, and agony depicted in every lineament of her handsome face." But "not even the shrewdest and most careful observer" could see "a twitch of a muscle . . . a downcast look . . . [or] any movement indicative of remorse or . . . guilt" by the accused man.[23]

"Last time I saw my parents and brothers alive was two weeks before they were found dead," Maude told a hushed courtroom. "I found them dead at my brother's home February 24; a driver went with me[,] it was dusk, and [it] was dark inside the house; [I] tried the door of the east room [and] couldn't open it. . . . I called my brother, then went to [the] back door; the east room was all right; [I] went to the inside door of [the] west room in the entry [and] pushed it partly open [and] saw my mother on the floor; tried to get in [and I] don't know what happened after."[24]

She said her father was nearly sixty years old, and her mother was fifty-three. Ward was twenty-six; Fay, nineteen; John, seventeen; and Lemmie was thirteen. She had not seen the boys since the tenth or eleventh of February. There were three double-barreled shotguns on the farm, she said, because her father, whom she described as "a small-sized man," and all of her brothers hunted ducks and birds.[25]

She recognized a clock that had been found in the buggy in Lake Charles as belonging to her brother Ward because of a string attached to it that she said in later testimony was used to hang it on his bedstead. She also testified that she had been in Bell's Store in Welsh when Ed Batson came in to purchase shotgun cartridges. She and Mary Robertson, another clerk at Bell's store, testified that Batson had come into the store "about the 10th," three weeks before the crime was discovered, and asked for 12-gauge shotgun shells loaded with BBs. There were none in stock, so Batson took the largest shells the store had.[26]

It is interesting that there was no testimony by the livery driver who could pick up where Maude's memory failed about what happened at Ward Earll's farm, the hasty dash back to Welsh, and the summoning of officers to the scene.

Several other witnesses testified about the last time they saw the victims; others were put on the stand with the intention of placing Ed Batson as close to the scene of the crime as possible and of tracing his route from Welsh into Lake Charles to sell Ward Earll's stock—a trip Batson claimed he could not have taken because he was already in Texas.

It was essential to establish that trail because the circumstantial case against Ed Batson rested heavily on the contention that he was the man who tried to sell the stock to John Downs. If Batson was not linked firmly to the stock, and the stock was not proven to be from the Earll farm, there was no case, circumstantial or otherwise.

Welsh resident R. P. Willard testified that he had seen Ward Earll alive at midmorning on February 12, and there appeared to be nothing unusual about him. Teacher Nettie Redeke said that "[Lemmie] Earle was at school Wednesday February 12; left in the afternoon when school was out; and he never returned."[27]

Another Welsh resident, W. A. Rodgers, testified he had seen Ward and L. S. Earll on February 12 when they paid a bill they owed and that he had seen Ed Batson wearing a black coat and a pair of overalls at the Southern Pacific depot in Lake Charles about midnight on February 14. He said he remembered the dates because he referred to his books to refresh his memory after the bodies were found. The fact that he had refreshed his memory brought a challenge by the defense, and the judge told the jury to disregard testimony concerning the dates.[28]

John LeBlanc, who lived between Welsh and the town of Iowa, said he saw Ed Batson between four and five o'clock in the afternoon of February 13, driving on the public road toward Lake Charles about three and a half miles from Ward Earll's house. LeBlanc said the accused man was in a buggy with a top on it, "driving two bay mules, leading two gray mules, a black and a bay horse." LeBlanc said he knew the black horse and gray mules belonged to Ward Earll. "I saw him plainly," the witness said. "He was driving fast . . . about sixty yards from me." He said he remembered the date because he broke a plow the next day, which was Valentine's Day.[29] It should be noted that LeBlanc told newspaper reporters in February that he had seen the horses pulling the wagon with the mules behind, but he testified at the trial that the mules were in harness and the horses were being led.[30]

"When I saw Batson that day," he testified, "I thought it was Earle; I had been thinking of trading horses with Earle, and ran out to hail him; I then saw it was not him and returned to the house." LeBlanc said he knew Ward's hired man because he had stayed in Earll's barn while baling hay and was "with him [Earll] and Batson every night for more than a week."[31]

Iowa saloon keeper Lastie Hebert said Ed Batson came into his place between seven and eight o'clock one night in February and paid fifty cents for a pint of whiskey. Hebert said Batson wanted to know where the nearest road to Lake Charles was because he had some horses and mules to take there. "I cannot remember the day of the month," he testified, "it was after Mardi Gras."[32]

Under questioning by the defense, Hebert insisted that Batson was the man who'd come to his saloon. He said Batson had been in the town of Iowa several times before, accompanying Ward Earll when he hauled rice into Iowa. The saloon keeper said, "[I] never have mistaken one man for another in my life." But he also admitted he did not know the name of the man who'd come to Iowa with Ward Earll and that, in fact, he had not known Ward Earll's name until someone told him who the two of them were. Judge Miller "instructed the jury to disregard entirely the identification of Ward Earle from what Mr. Hebert had learned from other people."[33]

A. J. Findlay was one of the most important of the witnesses relied on by the prosecution to trace Ed Batson's trail from the murder scene to the livery stable in Lake Charles. The irrigation canal superintendent from the town of Iowa testified that on the night of February 13, Ed Batson came to his house and asked to put up his stock in Findlay's barn and sleep there. He said he'd never seen Batson before that night.[34]

"I noticed the teams," Findlay told the court. "There was a small pair of light brown mules, a span of gray mules and a pair of bay horses. . . . He also had an ordinary top buggy." He said that on the morning of February 14, Batson paid the bill for the night and tried to sell him the two smaller mules.[35]

Jim Glover, a black man who worked for Findlay and who also spent the same night in the barn, said Batson told him he was going to meet a partner in Lake Charles and they were going to the town of Vinton near the Texas border to haul logs. He also testified that during the night Batson cried out, "Eh, there! Have you got a gun?"[36]

Another Iowa resident, Thomas Jones, said he'd seen Batson driving across a railroad crossing in the town on the morning of February 14, riding in a buggy pulled by mules, with two other mules and two horses being led. The men did not speak to each other.[37]

From Welsh to Iowa to Lake Charles—that was the route the prosecution claimed Ed Batson took to the livery barn where someone tried to sell Ward Earll's stock.

15

Batson's Turn

Through the early stages of his trial, Ed Batson appeared to be a calm, dispassionate, almost disinterested observer of the proceedings, but as the prosecution witnesses paraded to the stand, adding layer upon layer to the case, news reporters thought he began to appear more concerned about the way things were going—perhaps coming to the realization that as circumstantial as the evidence was, a case could be made against him that a willing jury might accept.

"The strain of the long trial is beginning to tell on Batson," the *Lake Charles Weekly American* reported.

> He has lost to some extent the air of serenity and confidence he wore when it began. Yesterday, while the state was piling up evidence of his presence in Lake Charles, Batson was calmly correcting a plat a newspaper man had made of Ward Earle's house and showing the position of the furniture; but, as the day wore on he took more interest in the evidence and frequently conferred with his counsel.
>
> This morning the youthful prisoner followed the evidence closely . . . and did not permit his attention to wander from it. No man in his position, whether guilty or innocent, could fail to understand the terrible significance of the network of evidence woven about him and it is only human for him to show his appreciation of it.[1]

J. Ed Ryan was the first of the prosecution witnesses to identify Ed Batson as the man who had come into Lake Charles on Valentine's Day and tried unsuccessfully to sell him some horses and mules. Ryan told the jury he first saw the man prosecutors claimed to be Batson about noon on February 14 when he drove up to Ryan's livery stable with four mules and two horses.[2] "He wanted to sell me the smaller pair of mules," Ryan testified. "I offered to trade for them; he refused to trade and went down the street with his stock." He said Batson wanted $225 for the span of mules, which Ryan found to have "a number" of barbwire cuts on them.[3]

Ben Johnson, a Ryan stable hand, said he also remembered Batson. He said Batson wanted to sell a span of iron-gray mules. "He talked sale and trade both," the witness said, "couldn't tell what he wanted to do." R. J. Gunn, proprietor of a stationery store across from Ryan's, said he saw Batson at the stable about noon on February 14.[4]

According to the prosecution's case, Batson was unable to sell the mules to Ed Ryan, so he took the stock to John Downs's stable to try to make a deal there. According to Downs's testimony,

> He drove up with a top buggy and a pair of small mules, leading two gray mules on either side, and behind a brown horse and a bay horse. . . . Mr. Oliver, a horse dealer was present when I spoke to the prisoner. . . . He was still in the buggy when I approached him and looked at the mules. . . . He said he wanted $225 for the gray mules. . . . I found that one mule had a very lame foot, which he said had been caused by a blacksmith forgetting to shoe the foot. I offered him $175 for the team; he would not accept the sum at first but finally concluded to do so. . . . I then asked him where he came from and he responded from [the] Paul Daniels canal in the Lacassine country; he had been rice farming on the canal but failed on account of the lack of water. He told me he had no water and to search out his meaning. I asked him did he have to steal it by cutting levees [and] he said, "You're dam[n] right." He gave his name as Earle and told me I could telephone Mr. Daniels and have him come over and identify the stock.[5]

Downs said he gave the man permission to put up his stock "and then took him up town to the Wells-Fargo Express office to allow him to send a box to Texas." The office was closed, but they met the express wagon on their way back to the stables, and the man got out of Downs's buggy and handed the box to the express driver.[6]

Orrin Mason, the express driver, testified later that the box was to be sent to a Kay Payne, in Spickard, Missouri, but could not identify Ed Batson as the man who gave the box to him. The name "Kay" could have been a mistake by the driver or a typographical error in the newspaper report of the trial. Rachel Payne was sometimes called "Rae," which could easily be confused with Kay. As we have seen, the box was delivered to her, although no testimony to that fact was introduced at the trial. Mason testified that he remembered receiving a box on February 14 from a man riding with John Downs but that he could not positively identify the stranger.[7]

"He asked me if there was a gunsmith in town," Downs continued, "and I directed him to the old man whose shop is just north of Sam Kaufman's implement store. The last time I saw the accused [that day] he was in front of Martin Klawe's blacksmith shop on Ryan Street, eating candy or peanuts." Downs said he did not call Paul Daniels that day to come identify the stock, and sixteen days later he turned the stock over to a man named Jesse Hutchins. Downs testified that the next time he saw Ed Batson was in the jail yard in New Orleans about March 15. He said he could definitely identify him as the same man because of a scar on his face.[8]

Downs testified that he kept the Earll stock for more than two weeks before Fred Earll told him to turn over the animals to Jesse Hutchins. Hutchins testified that he took the animals back to Welsh and put them in the care of liveryman Henry Daigle.[9]

W. K. Oliver next took the oath and testified that he traded horses and mules from a barn next to Downs's stable and reiterated Downs's testimony. He said also that he saw the prisoner sitting in the buggy writing something and that he saw the muzzle of a shotgun sticking out of the buggy.[10]

Gunsmith D. C. Williamson testified that a man who gave his name as C. R. Batson brought a shotgun to him on

February 14 wanting a new trigger guard for it. Williamson said, "I refused to make one as I was too busy. . . . Some blacksmith had made the old trigger guard." He said he could not identify Batson as the man who came into his shop. That man, he said "came to the shop about 4 o'clock in the afternoon; it was dark. [I was] unable to recognize the man as he stood between me and the light; his face was darkened . . . and the right side was turned toward me."[11]

Williamson said the man never came back for the gun, and it remained in his shop until Fred Earll, the only surviving son, came to identify it days later. Neither he nor the prosecutors gave any reason why the stranger used the name C. R. Batson or why he began using that name when he had earlier claimed to be Ward Earll.[12]

Fred Earll was the next witness to take the oath; his testimony was not as wrenching as his sister's, but was potentially more damning. He said he first learned of the death of his relatives on February 25 and that he left that day from Mount Eagle, Iowa, to come to Lake Charles, reaching the town on Friday, February 28. He went to Downs's stable on Saturday morning, where he recognized the black horse and the gray mules as belonging to his brother Ward. He also went to the gunsmith's and picked from eleven others a shotgun that belonged to his brother Fay.[13]

Verifying the account by gunsmith D. C. Williamson that the trigger guard on the shotgun left in Lake Charles was handmade, Fred Earll said J. D. Kimble, a blacksmith in Welsh, had done the work. Defense attorneys objected to any testimony about the shotgun, arguing that prosecutors had not connected it in any way to the case. The objection was overruled and the testimony allowed.[14]

Fred testified, as had his sister, Maude, that Ward owned a gold Hampden watch.[15] Lake Charles jeweler Otto Winterhalter testified after Fred that he knew the watch, having repaired it for Ward Earll in January 1901, and it was the same one brought to his shop for repair by a man giving the name of A. E. Batson on February 14, 1902. The jeweler said he fixed a broken mainspring on the watch and that the man returned for it the same day.[16]

Again there is no explanation of why the stranger—presuming he was the same man who tried to sell the mules and have a shotgun repaired—changed his name from Ward Earll to C. R. Batson to A. E. Batson.

Will Martin, the next prosecution witness, said he saw Batson "about the twelfth or thirteenth of February" at the Downs stable. Martin said he recognized a black horse that belonged to Ward Earll but that Batson told him the horse no longer belonged to Earll.[17]

The next bit of testimony would prove pivotal in Ed Batson's first trial. When the state attempted to introduce the Ha-Ha letter into evidence, characterizing it as a suicide note, the defense objected because it had not been shown that Batson wrote it nor that the handwriting on it was his. The judge allowed the letter into evidence but told the jury its introduction did not mean it had been written by the defendant, and the jurors could decide for themselves on its authenticity.[16]

The defense also objected to the state's attempt to show that Batson wrote the note that was tacked to Ward Earll's door. Since prosecutors had no handwriting sample that could positively be identified as Batson's to use for comparison, and the defendant refused to give one, they tried to prove that Ward Earll had not written the notice on the door so, therefore, it must have been written by the killer, whom as far as the prosecution was concerned was Batson.

In his legal analysis, Underwood wrote:

> There was some interesting if confusing testimony regarding the handwriting on various exhibits. The object of the exercise was to show that the note left on the door . . . [was] not written by Ward Earle but . . . instead . . . by someone else, presumably Batson, who had put it on the door to keep away the inquisitive, to give him a chance to make tracks. . . . The prosecution first tendered a grocer by the name of Jo. C. Elstner as a handwriting expert, but he was not properly qualified and his testimony was

> excluded. The prosecution had more luck with the testimony of Frank A. Roberts, the cashier of Calcasieu Bank, a man who was well practiced in the observation of signatures. He testified that the same hand . . . wrote the note on the door . . . and also wrote the "Ha Ha letter."[18]

That was the last of the significant testimony, and after recalling several witnesses to clean up one or two details, the prosecution rested its case against Ed Batson at 3:15 P.M. on Friday, April 18.[19]

Forty-five minutes later, the defense put on the stand its only major witness: Albert Edwin Batson. Ed Batson's defense attorneys, earnest but inexperienced in criminal law, apparently thought the circumstantial case presented by the state failed to place their client at the scene of the crime, failed to put a murder weapon in his hands, and failed to offer a convincing motive for him to kill six people.[20]

It has been suggested that this was the reason the defense did not present the most vigorous case it could. There also seemed to be a question of money to finance finding witnesses, bringing them to Lake Charles, and paying for the court-appointed defense attorneys' time.

Batson's lawyers, for example, did not call to the stand railroad employees who had told the press they had seen Ed Batson on a train heading north from Beaumont at about the same time prosecution witnesses said he was driving stock through Iowa toward Lake Charles. Neither did they call the men who made mistaken identifications in the jail yard, nor did they examine any of the men Batson said he'd seen in Welsh on his way out of town. The defense did, however, bring to the courtroom P. A. Emmett, whom Batson recognized as a barber from Vinton, where he said he'd stopped on his way to Beaumont; Pierre Chaison, who said he saw Batson in Vinton; and a waiter who worked in a Vinton restaurant where Batson said he had dinner. According to the *St. Louis Republic*, "These persons, while not able to testify positively that Batson had met them, believed that he . . . had dealt with them as claimed."[21]

In the end, however, the defense attorneys believed the cool, collected, well-spoken young man would be the best witness for himself. "The testimony of the accused was entirely unexpected by everybody," the *Lake Charles Weekly American* reported, "yet when he commenced to speak a hush fell upon the crowd; when he resumed his seat beside his devoted mother the vast crowd was dazed."[22]

Underwood notes that the defense was very careful about what it asked Ed Batson on the theory that the cross-examination could not address anything that was not covered in direct testimony. He wrote, "All the cross-examiner got was Batson's insistence that he had left Ward's place around nine in the morning on February 12, and headed for Missouri, and his denial that he killed each of the victims as the prosecutor read each of their names to him."[23]

According to the *Weekly American*,

> Batson's appearance on the stand was cool and unshaken; he never quailed, not a nerve in his body quivered. His eyes were steady, his countenance had not shadowed to any great degree, his gaze was firm and in answering the last questions . . . that involved his life he looked the District Attorney squarely in the eye and gave his answers in a clear, smooth tone of voice. Not at any moment was he excited or uncollected. When he had responded to the final question put by the state, he looked at the jury—not in a casual manner for a few seconds.
>
> Batson is a remarkable young man; he is contented and cheerful and braves the penetrating arrows of the law with wonderful coolness and stability.[24]

The questions by his attorneys went right to the point:

> "What is your name?"
> "My name is A. E. Batson."
> "Did you know Ward Earle?"
> "I did."
> "Did you ever live with Ward Earle?"
> "I lived in the same house with him."

"When did you leave there?"

"I left on February 12."

"Did you kill any members of the Earle family?"

"I did not, sir."

"Were you implicated directly or indirectly in the killing of the Earles?"

"I was not."[25]

Cross-examination by the prosecution was equally to the point:

"You did not kill Ward Earle?"

"No, sir; I did not."

"You did not kill Fay Earle?"

"No, sir; I did not."

"You did not kill little Lemuel Earle?"

"No, sir; I did not."

"You did not kill John Earle?"

"No, sir; I did not."

"You did not kill old man Earle?"

"No, sir; I did not."

"You did not kill Mrs. Earle?"

"No, sir; I did not."

"You are positive of that?"

"I am, sir."[26]

With that, the defense rested, and after a brief recess, the court adjourned until Saturday morning, when final arguments would be made.

16

Reaching a Verdict

In the end, Ed Batson's fate may have been sealed as much by oratory as by evidence. At least that is the view presented in Underwood's analysis of the trial. "As far as closing arguments," he writes, "the defense efforts were no match for the powerful and emotional closing argument of prosecutor Mitchell. Fairly or unfairly, properly or not, he criticized Batson for limiting his testimony on the stand to a 'mere' denial of the murders, and for giving no explanation for his possession of the mules, the watch, and other property—[saying] 'No innocent man would have acted in that manner.'"[1]

From the time of his arrest, Batson had denied not only that he killed anyone but also that he was ever in possession of the mules, the watch, or other property.

The courtroom was packed as the prosecution and defense made their final arguments on Saturday morning, and "ladies predominated in the audience," according to the press.[2] The *Lake Charles Weekly American* reporter wrote, "The jury was in their places [*sic*] early. A few minutes before the hour arrived, Batson came in accompanied by his faithful escort [of sheriff's deputies], and at once became the center of attraction. The sound of the clanking steel, as his handcuffs were removed, sent a shiver over the fair portion of the audience. Batson was not discomposed in the slightest degree by the attention he attracted. He sat down and greeted his counsel with a smile. The attorneys looked much more worried than he."[3]

Mitchell opened his remarks for the prosecution by thanking the jury for its attention and patience, then told the jurors that in their hands "lay not only the fate of the accused, but the safety of their fellow citizens." He "painted in strong language the enormity of the crime as one without parallel," calling the crime "atrocious" and "inexcusable" and "without a shadow of palliation." Then, after going over the evidence presented by the state, he turned to the self-possessed Batson as he told the jurors, "His very conduct, his indifference, his hardness prove his guilt." The prosecutor said there was only one possible verdict.[4]

For its part, the defense urged the jurors to look at the evidence impartially and to recognize that the case presented by the state failed to prove Batson committed the crime. Defense attorney Sompayrac told jurors, "We do not appeal for mercy, but ask the jury not to yield to abuse but to judge the evidence impartially."[5]

He said, "Two things are necessary to prove a murder. . . . The motive is one. Unless a motive was shown, either the man was innocent or insane. The state has failed to prove a motive. It is ridiculous to think that [Ed Batson] would commit such a crime to steal [some] mules." Nor was money the motive, he said. "Ward Earle had no money . . . and the accused knew it." He argued the state had failed to prove Batson was the man who brought Ward Earll's mules to Lake Charles and cited court decisions showing the ease with which people can be misidentified. He said unless Batson was proven to be in possession of the mules, there was no case against him, and the state had not shown beyond doubt that Ed Batson was the man seen in Lake Charles. "The evidence has not that absolute certainty required in cases of circumstantial evidence," he said.[6]

The second defense attorney, Overton, said there was no denying "that a most horrible crime had been committed," but there was also no denying there was no real proof it was committed by his client. "The mere appearance of guilt is not enough," he argued, "the state must show that [the] circumstances must be capable of no other explanation than the guilt of the accused."[7]

Overton said the chain of evidence presented by the state had too many missing links and reiterated that the evidence presented by the prosecution did not even prove Ed Batson was the man with the mules in Lake Charles, let alone the murderer of six people. The state had tied possession of the mules to the murderer, he said, but even if Batson was the man with the mules, "the inference that he stole [the stock] might be proper, but not the inference of murder."[8]

With the end of the defense arguments, the court recessed until 1:30 P.M., when District Attorney Moore made the final argument for the prosecution, reminding the jurors that at the time of their selection they were instructed that they could convict on circumstantial evidence. He argued that such evidence is "not only perfectly legal evidence, but is often more conclusive than direct evidence." As his conclusion, he read the law concerning capital punishment to the jury.[9]

Judge Miller began reading his instructions to the jury a little before 3:00 P.M. on Saturday, telling the jurors Ed Batson had to be proven guilty beyond a reasonable doubt and that if the jury "found any hypothesis incompatible with the guilt of the accused they must acquit him."[10] The jury retired at 3:20 P.M., and Judge Miller told them that since it was a Saturday, he wanted them to deliberate for three hours to see if they could reach a verdict. He did not want to keep them into the night.

A crowd lingered around the courthouse waiting to see what would happen. According to Charles Dobson's account, "When half an hour had passed without a verdict . . . the crowd grew impatient, some congregated under the window of the jury room and indicated their displeasure by curses, waving of handkerchiefs, and in fact their conduct caused counsel for the defendant to appeal to the Judge to order them dispersed."[11]

As the three hours allocated for Saturday deliberation neared an end, Judge Miller sent Chief Deputy Richard to see if there was any chance of a verdict. The officer went to the door of the jury room, whispered words with someone inside, and then had a private conversation with the judge. Nobody heard what the deputy said, but Judge Miller left the bench and returned to his chambers, sending speculation through the crowd that a verdict was about to come.

Ten minutes later a knock on the door sounded from inside the jury room, but the *Weekly American* reported, "It only meant fresh disappointment. The jury was preparing to take a ballot when Mr. Richard first applied for information, but it showed no agreement, and court at once adjourned, the judge adhering to his policy of risking no night sessions on this case."[12]

The first vote taken that Saturday evening was later reported to be ten votes to convict, two to acquit. As the deliberation continued, the two jurors who voted for acquittal apparently agreed to vote for a guilty verdict, but they held out for some time because they wanted a sentence of life in prison rather than the death penalty.[13]

The decision that Ed Batson would hang for the Earll murders became unanimous sometime on Sunday morning. "It is known that the verdict was agreed upon before noon Sunday," the *Weekly American* reported, "because at that hour the jury sent a message to that effect to Judge Miller."[14]

And so it was generally known the jury had already reached a verdict when court reconvened at 9:00 A.M. on Monday, April 21. Prosecutors and defense attorneys were at their places by 8:45 A.M. Batson's mother took her usual place just a few minutes later, her face pale and showing strain.[15]

"A hush fell upon the court room as Batson, handcuffed as usual, came in with Sheriff Perkins and escorted by a half dozen deputies who ranged themselves immediately behind his chair. The courtroom, in fact, was alive with officers," the newspaper reported. The sheriff evidently intended to take no chances either with the prisoner or with the audience.

> Batson was rather pale and much graver than usual, but was as self-possessed as ever. He exchanged a few words with his attorneys, then leaned over to his mother who whispered to him the agitating news that the verdict would probably be against him. He showed no sign of emotion or nervousness other than a certain restlessness. He would rock the vacant chair in front of him for awhile then would tilt himself back in his own chair and rock back and forth.[16]

Judge Miller called the court to order promptly at 9:00 A.M., and the jury was brought in after a few preliminaries.

"Gentlemen of the Jury, have you agreed upon a verdict?" the judge asked.

"We have, your Honor," replied jury foreman Paul Sullivan, handing a slip of paper to the chief deputy. He handed it to the judge, who, after reading it, handed it to clerk of court H. C. Gill. It read: "We, the jury, find the accused guilty as charged."[17]

"Batson turned white as the words which carried a message of death to him were read, but not a muscle quivered," the *Weekly American* reporter wrote. "People who were close to him thought they detected moisture in his eyes. Mrs. Payne pressed her handkerchief to her eyes once or twice but bore the grievous news like a Spartan mother. . . . Sheriff Perkins and Deputy Hartman moved a little closer to the prisoner."[18]

The jurors were polled one by one, each saying he agreed with the verdict, without "doubt or hesitation." They were then discharged, and "the youthful prisoner, still pale but firm, meekly held out his hands for the manacles." Deputies crowded around him but "opened a way for his poor mother, her handkerchief still nervously clasped between her fingers, to approach and try to comfort him. A number of ladies wept as the prisoner, handcuffed to Deputies Hartman and Lyons, was led out under heavy guard. And those outside presently saw emerge from the building and walk slowly up the side street, a broken-hearted woman, friendless even in that hour of bitterness."[19] Rachel Payne was apparently alone in her grief.

"It is almost needless to say that the verdict against Batson meets the almost unanimous approval of the people of this community," the *Weekly American* reported. "While they have the greatest sympathy for the prisoner's mother, there is little compassion for Batson, in view of the horrible nature of the crime for which he has been convicted. Any other verdict would have been looked upon as a miscarriage of justice."[20]

Maude Earll, who had been so distraught during her testimony, celebrated the verdict by getting married that same day to painter and paperhanger Charles K. Ingram of Orange, Texas.[21]

Attorneys for the defense were given two weeks to file the expected (and denied) motions for a new trial and to clear up other sundries. Only a handful of spectators were present in the courtroom on May 3, when Ed Batson's sentence was imposed. He was instructed to stand and was asked if he could offer any reason why he should not be sentenced. Composed as always, he replied quietly but firmly, "No, nothing, except that I am innocent."[22]

The judge's voice "grew husky with emotion" as he spoke the fateful words: "It is considered and adjudged and this court sentences you, A. E. Batson, to be remanded to the parish jail and there safely kept until such day as the governor may fix; and then by the proper officer to be conveyed to the place prepared for your execution, and then and there to be hanged by the neck until you are dead, dead, dead.

And [may] God have mercy upon your soul."[23]

17

A Ray of Hope and an Appeal

Only days after Ed Batson's conviction, his attorney Paul Sompayrac was on a train headed for the southeastern Louisiana town of Clinton, about thirty miles north of Baton Rouge, where a man named Tom Jackson was said to have confessed that he was the one who killed the Earlls. Batson's attorneys also immediately appealed the verdict to the Louisiana Supreme Court, primarily on technical points that Underwood argues "even a legal observer at the time might have thought were unlikely to secure a reversal."[1]

The train ride was a long shot. Authorities in Clinton gave little credence to the confession and thought Jackson was insane. But a Lake Charles man who knew the confessor said he had a scar on his face similar to Ed Batson's, and the *Houston Daily Post* reported Jackson had returned to Clinton with eight hundred dollars in his pocket after being away for several months. Further, "within an hour of his return he met his brother and shot him dead with no known provocation."[2]

A reporter for the *Jennings Daily Record* wrote that after Jackson was arrested for shooting his brother "and after being placed in prison a short time made the statement to the legal authorities that he was the murderer of the Earll family for which A. E. Batson had been convicted."[3] According to the story, Sheriff Perkins was also going to Clinton "and will bring Jackson to Lake Charles for trial and [he] will be given a preliminary hearing next Monday."[4] There is no further report of Perkins going to Clinton or of a hearing in Lake Charles.

Indeed, the Clinton authorities proved to be right; the trip taken by Paul Sompayrac proved to be futile. The confession was bogus, Jackson was not the Earlls' killer.

The writer of the Jennings article had also apparently smelled something fishy with the Clinton story. "The [report from Clinton] may be only a rumor," the newspaper concluded, "but there is nothing unreasonable in the statement made, and furthermore there are many people who believe Batson innocent. If this report proves true it will be a hard blow to circumstantial evidence and mob law."[5]

With the discounting of the Jackson "confession," the onus now fell to Sompayrac's partner in the defense, Winston Overton, who argued before the Louisiana Supreme Court on Saturday, June 8, that his client deserved a new trial. District attorney Joseph Moore and attorney general Walter Guion represented the prosecution.[6] As Batson's lawyers had argued before his trial, the defense claimed the duplication of a name in the list of potential grand jurors caused that list to be one name short, which meant the grand jury that indicted Ed Batson was illegally constituted.

In the majority opinion of the Louisiana Supreme Court handed down on June 21, 1902, Justice Frank A. Monroe said that didn't make any difference "in the absence of fraud or actual injury."[7]

The defense also challenged the indictment itself, arguing it was improper to lump six murders into one indictment and that Ed Batson should have been charged separately for each of the six deaths.

According to a news account, Overton "argued at great length . . . offering numerous authorities in support of his contention, showing that the charging of Batson in one count with the murder of six people was in violation of a rule of criminal pleading that prevailed in Roman law, common law, has found lodgment in the penal codes of many states of the union, and is firmly established in the jurisprudence of Louisiana and her sister states."[8]

The argument fell on deaf ears. Justice Monroe upheld the indictment, writing that

> the view suggested by the learned and zealous counsel who, by appointment of the court, have defended the accused, is not without support, [but] the weight of authority, and of reason, sustains the proposition that though a criminal act may operate upon more than one person or thing . . . so long as it is one act, consummated at one time, it may be charged as one offense. . . . The charge as made is . . . in strict accordance with the [law] and there is nothing . . . to indicate that the persons named were not killed at the same instant and by the same act. . . . If, however, the testimony shows that the killing of two persons was not one act, the defendant has the right to compel the state to select upon which charge it will proceed. . . . It does not appear that the state was called on to make such an election.[9]

The court apparently did not consider the murder of L. S. Earll a separate offense, even though the elder man was slain away from the cabin where the others were killed. The majority of the court also found that the defense's charge of errors made in jury selection were "not well founded"; the district court judge was correct in allowing testimony by John Downs, which the defense questioned as hearsay; and that most of the other defense complaints were without merit.[10]

But two of the three members of the Louisiana Supreme Court accepted the defense argument that introduction of a deed bearing Ward Earll's signature was not proper. The deed was part of the evidence used in an attempt to show that someone other than Earll had written the note affixed to his door at the time of the murders. Prosecutors claimed Batson wrote that note, but they did not have a sample of his handwriting to prove it in court. Instead, they used a deed that Ward Earll had signed, trying to show that the handwriting on the deed differed from the writing on the note on the door, and thus, by inference, the note had to be written by the killer—that is, Ed Batson.

Relying on an obscure and technical point found first in English common law, the supreme court decided the deed and testimony about the deed was not proper. The high court threw out Ed Batson's guilty verdict and decreed that a new trial had to be held. According to the majority opinion, "The writing offered to the jury . . . was not admissible, and the defendant has been convicted upon illegal evidence."[11]

The vote on the Louisiana Supreme Court was two to one; justice Joseph A. Breaux dissented in that opinion, and Underwood agreed with this dissent, writing:

> For this illogical [decision], the majority of the court relied upon English common law cases. Justice Breaux quite properly dissented, pointing out that the English rule in the cases relied upon by the majority had been overturned by statute in England, and should not be followed in this case. In other words, Batson's conviction was reversed on a technicality, and a technicality that would make no sense to the modern lawyer. If there was a conspiracy against Batson, the Supreme Court of Louisiana was apparently not in on it, and one wonders if the majority were not fishing for any reason to set aside the death sentence.[12]

Whatever the arguments, and reasons for them, Ed Batson was given a second chance to prove his innocence.

The *Lake Charles Weekly American* reported, "It was past 6 o'clock Saturday evening when Attorney Winston Overton . . . received a telegram from the clerk of the Supreme Court, announcing Batson's good fortune. It was past the hour for gaining admission to the jail, but Mr. Overton sent word to his client. Jailer Lyons was present when Batson learned that the shadow of death had been lifted from him. The doomed-young man, for once, lost his iron composure and showed his joy and relief over the action of the court."[13]

During the time taken up by the appeal, however, significant renovations were being made to the courthouse in Lake Charles, and that meant Ed Batson would have to wait for the carpenters to finish their work before he went back into the courtroom. "I will bring Batson to trial again at the earliest possible moment," the district attorney told the press after the supreme court pronouncement. "We are all torn up at the courthouse now. It would be impossible to conduct a case of this magnitude in the temporary building."[14]

District Attorney Moore had hoped to begin the second trial in September, but that date proved to be optimistic. On September 27 Batson attorney Winston Overton told the press that the second trial would have to wait at least until December and possibly longer, as "the parish is building a new courthouse and the old one is out of commission." Sheriff Perkins said, "For the time being court is sitting in a temporary structure erected on the grounds, but it would not be sufficiently substantial for a murder trial with sensational features as that of Batson's." According to the newspaper account, the sheriff didn't like the idea of holding the trial in the temporary building because "there would be no protection in case public feeling should become excited and intensified during the trial."[15]

Meanwhile, the defendant was spending his time leisurely reading books as he awaited his next date with judge and jury.[16] The *Welsh Rice Belt Journal* made note of Batson's new taste for reading: "Batson has become an incessant reader of books since his death sentence. He reads all the time. He lies in the steel cage and peruses the pages of thrilling novels. . . . He eats breakfast in the morning, and then takes up his book. It is the same thing day in and day out."[17] This was a new habit, according to the report, which continued, "Batson formerly never read. He did not like print; and he did not even follow all of his case in the papers."[18]

According to the newspaper report, women from Calcasieu Parish "provide him with the rarest of literature and he wades through it. . . . But if the story isn't thrilling it doesn't catch Batson and he lays down the volume. You would be surprised to see the latest novels of the day . . . in Ed Batson's cell. He likes detective stories and tales of thrilling adventure."[19]

The regimen seemed to agree with him.

"During the time the death sentence was hanging fire in the Supreme court Batson was confined in the death cell, and he grew pale and thin," the reporter wrote. "But since [he was] again placed in the steel inclosure [*sic*] he has gained in weight and is devoting all of his time to literature. . . . Curious people still want to see the noted prisoner, and the sheriff has found it necessary to set regular visiting days and to abide by them strictly. Otherwise there would be a continual string of people going to the jail merely to get a look at Batson. He doesn't mind the onlookers and reads while they peer through the cage."[20]

Calcasieu authorities seemed to take an ambivalent attitude about this accused killer of six people, guarding him zealously in the courtroom and in his short trips from cell to court, yet letting practically anyone parade past his cell to point and gawk so they could tell their grandchildren they'd seen the notorious Batson.

18

To Court Again

When the Louisiana Supreme Court ordered a new trial for Ed Batson, his attorneys immediately filed a motion to have it held someplace other than Lake Charles. The defense attorneys said they were "very anxious" for a change of the trial site because they thought that "[if they had] a change of venue, the life of Batson could at least be saved."[1]

So it was that in mid-December 1902, "a number of attorneys and a sprinkling of spectators" were on hand as a trio of deputies led Ed Batson "into the frameshack doing duty as a courthouse" for testimony to answer the question posed in a front-page headline of the *Lake Charles Daily American*: "Can Batson Get Fair Play Here?"[2]

Forty witnesses were called over two days to try to provide an answer, and not surprisingly, most of them concluded that a fair trial could be held in Lake Charles and that Batson would be acquitted if he could prove his innocence. The hearing went on even though defense attorney Winston Overton said his and his associate counsel's health "had prevented them from properly working for the change of venue."[3] Typical was the testimony of the first witness, W. R. Norris, who, according to the press reports, said he believed "people had made up their minds that Batson is guilty and that he ought to suffer for his guilt," but that he would still receive a "fair and just trial in the parish." Under cross-examination, Norris said, "Calcasieu juries have always been fair and even partial toward accused persons; people have made no demonstration against Batson and will make none; he is perfectly safe; all excitement and feeling has subsided."[4]

Dr. L. C. Anderson was less positive about how fair-minded a Calcasieu Parish jury might be. He said it would be "impractical and perhaps impossible to get a jury of twelve men in Calcasieu Parish who would give the accused a fair and impartial trial." Merchant Luc LeDoux, of the town of Oberlin, testified that he'd heard people in the crowd who were awaiting the first verdict say they would lynch Batson if he was acquitted.[5]

But theirs was a minority opinion. Aladin Vincent, a wealthy landowner from the Vinton area, testified that "he believed not only one but several juries of Calcasieu men could be obtained who would [put aside] any opinions they might have and give the accused a fair and impartial trial [based on the evidence]."[6]

Regarding the question of Batson's safety in Calcasieu Parish, deputy sheriff C. M. Richard testified that at the urging of Governor Heard, authorities had taken precautions against any lynching attempt but "he could not recollect that [any such attempt] had been reported as being contemplated." His testimony was seconded by deputy D. C. Lyons.[7]

As expected, Judge Miller ruled that a Calcasieu Parish jury sitting in Lake Charles could be fair and impartial and that no change of venue was necessary, partly because, according to the press, "the Batsons were unable to raise sufficient funds to defray the necessary cost of the court process."[8]

Ed Batson's second trial finally opened in a newly remodeled Calcasieu Parish courthouse at "a minute or so after two" on Friday, March 6, 1903.[9] The principals were the same as in the first trial: Judge Miller was on the bench, District Attorney Moore was again aided by A. R. Mitchell for the prosecution, and Paul Sompayrac and Winston Overton again sought to defend the accused.

Curious citizens again flocked to the courthouse, as they had for the first trial. "Although the case has been heard once and the evidence is probably little changed," the *Lake Charles Weekly American* reported, "a large audience was in the courtroom. It is evident that the capacity of the courtroom is going to be tested as the interest in the trial continues."[10]

"Excepting for a more convenient courtroom, there was little difference in the surroundings when the trial began," the *Weekly American* reported. "There was the same curious, but not hostile, crowd, eager to catch a glimpse of the man accused of such a frightful deed. A strong guard of deputy sheriffs was on hand, as in the first trial, but, there is no more reason for it now than there was then. While Calcasieu people abhor the crime and desire to see justice done . . . they are willing to be more than fair to the accused; and he is as safe here as he would be in his native Missouri hills."[11]

The defendant "took a seat on a bench in the west end of the room, just inside the railing. Deputies D. C. Lyons and Ike Fontenot sat down beside him just to keep him from getting lonesome, and other deputies kept nearby," according to the press.[12]

Although Batson had reportedly been sick the night before, he again showed no strain as the new trial began. He wore a dark suit, green tie, and glossy collar as he sat calmly watching the day's proceedings.[13] "It is hardly necessary to say that the imperturbable young man was cool and self-possessed," the *Weekly American* reported. "No one has ever seen him otherwise. His ruddy countenance shows scarcely a trace of his year's confinement in jail or the strain he has undergone." When his mother "was escorted to a seat beside her son," he greeted her "as warmly as usual and they were soon deep in conversation."[14] Rachel Payne never missed a day in court in either of her son's two trials.

Essentially, the same arguments used in the first trial were presented in the second one, but this time there was even less evidence. The gray vest the prosecution claimed was in Batson's buggy on the day he'd tried to trade Ward Earll's mules and a pair of bloody gloves were now missing. They had apparently been taken or misplaced when the evidence for the trial was moved during the construction work on the courthouse.

It took nearly three days to select an impartial jury willing to hang a man on only circumstantial evidence. As pointed out in the Welsh newspaper,

> From the beginning the prevailing opinion was that the selection of a jury was going to be a most difficult thing. Nearly everybody in the state who could read had read of the . . . Batson case, and had expressed opinions as to the guilt or innocence of the accused, and in the Parish of Calcasieu it was safe to say that everybody had read or heard of the case, and had discussed it, [and] hence would be incompetent to serve as jurors. It was also known that the defense would endeavor to keep any residents of Lake Charles or Welsh off the jury and that if they accepted any at all, it would be from out in the country.[15]

When it was finally selected, the second jury was composed of the following:

- S. E. A. Strother, who said he had heard about the case and formed no opinion on it but also said he would not convict solely on circumstantial evidence.
- Charles Delaney, who said he had no opinion about Batson's guilt or innocence and he would convict on circumstantial evidence.
- Allan Saunders, who said he would convict on circumstantial evidence "if it was strong enough."
- Jasper Stine, who told the court he could render a death verdict on circumstantial evidence.
- Theodule Breaux, who was "all right on capital punishment and circumstantial evidence" and said he could "disregard all he has heard and try the case on the law and the evidence."
- John Abney, who said he too could have no trouble giving a death verdict on circumstantial evidence.
- H. L. Shultz, who said he was not opposed to capital punishment.
- J. M. Simmons, who said he had no fixed opinion about guilt or innocence.
- James Hill, who said he had formed an opinion about guilt, but that it would "yield to evidence" and that "circumstantial evidence would be sufficient."

- Edwin Reynolds, who said he had no scruples about the death penalty.
- W. J. Pugh, who said he was "not biased against circumstantial evidence."
- J. M. Capps, who said he was in favor of capital punishment.[16]

At 1:40 P.M., on Tuesday, March 10, "District Attorney Moore read the indictment to the jury, in which Batson was charged with the murder of the Earl family. . . . [and] read the law bearing on the case. . . . Mr. Sompayrac . . . told the jury that the defendant pleads not guilty to the charge."[17]

The state then called forty witnesses, and the defense called thirteen, both sides asking that some of the witnesses be sequestered. Judge Miller approved a motion by the prosecution that "Mrs. Ingram [the former Maude Earll], Miss Nettie Radecke, Coroner Watkins, Marie Robinson and Deputies Lyons and Fontenot" would be allowed to remain in the courtroom, and a motion by the defense to allow "Mrs. Olsen, Rosa Styles, Judge [F. W.] Coon and M. Joy," to remain.[18]

With that, the first witness, Samuel Blackford, justice of the peace in Welsh, was called. As in the first trial, the prosecution began with witnesses who described the gory sixteen-square-foot room where the bodies of the Earll family were found. Blackford was followed by the coroner, Dr. Watkins, and by Deputy Fontenot and neighbors who had seen the carnage.[19]

They described the positions of the bodies, the wounds, and how the victims were dressed. They spoke about the general appearance of the room, seeing shot in the walls, and finding shotgun shells. Deputy Fontenot said he found a dead horse in the Earll stable and a "poor looking gray mule" that had eaten the bark off a China ball tree to stay alive.[20]

As more witnesses were called to the stand to describe the grisly scene, Sompayrac "suggested that as the trial was likely to be a long one, there seemed to be no need of prolonging it. The defense . . . did not dispute the death of these people and this line of testimony was merely cumulative. The state's attorney insisted, however, and [witness K. P. Willard, an Earll neighbor] went on and described the gruesome spectacle the charnel house presented."[21]

Maude Earll, who was now Mrs. Charles Ingram, gave a bit more detail in her testimony than she had at the first trial. She said that "someone from Lake Charles" had telephoned her to ask if she knew that Ward was going to Texas. "I replied that I did not," she told the court.

"He said I had better investigate," she continued, "as there was something wrong with Ward. . . . So, getting a livery rig I went to Ward's home. I tried all the doors on the north side and could not open them. I was calling Ward all the time. [I] went to a window and it was covered with oilcloth. . . . [then I] went around to the south side, opened the door, got a match from the driver, and asking him to come with me, went in and lit the lamp. Going to the door leading to the bedroom, I pulled it open and saw mother's face. I do not remember anything else."[22]

It was not reported if the defense attorneys pointed out that this testimony differs from Maude's account in the first trial. This time she says someone from Lake Charles called her. In the first trial, she said Welsh businessman Paul Daniels called.

Just as with the first trial, the driver who took Maude to the house and who rushed back to Welsh to report the crime was not called to pick up the story from where her memory failed. His name was not among potential witnesses, perhaps because prosecutors did not want his testimony to negate the emotional impact left by Maude's account.

Paul Daniels testified that contrary to the story the stranger at the livery stable told on February 14 of a failed crop, Ward Earll had raised "a good crop of rice of excellent quality" that year, and Daniels had bought some of it for about $700 to $800 and had also bought rice from L. S. Earll. He said he settled the account about two weeks before Ward was found dead, and that was the last time Daniels saw him alive.[23]

A. J. Findlay and another series of witnesses gave practically the same testimony as they had in the first trial, as the prosecuting attorneys tried to trace the route they claimed Ed Batson took from the Earll farm into Lake Charles. Findlay testified he was "positive" Batson was the man who stayed in his barn in the town of Iowa, midway between Welsh and Lake Charles.

"He had a span of gray mules, a bay horse and dark mares," Findlay said. "He had some clothing in his rig, also a shotgun. . . . Talking at the barn, [the man] said he had bought the mules at Jennings, paying $260 for them, that he lived above DeQuincy [a sawmill town north of Lake Charles] and was in the log business."[24]

Jim Glover, the black man who also stayed that night in Findlay's barn, testified that the stranger asked him if he had a gun because the stranger said he "wanted a little pocket gun." His testimony also was different from what he said in the first trial. Iowa saloon keeper Lastie Hebert and merchant L. L. Funk again testified that they had seen Batson in Iowa on February 14, 1902. "I remember that he came there on the 14th of February, because it was the day following my return from the New Orleans carnival," Funk said.[25]

When it came time to introduce evidence about the handwriting on the note left on Ward Earll's door, the prosecution was presented with the same dilemma that had been its undoing in the first trial. The state still could not reliably prove the handwriting on the document was Ed Batson's, so prosecutors again attempted to prove it was not Ward Earll's, leaving the implication that it had to have been written by the murderer. A technicality about that part of the first trial was the reason the Louisiana Supreme Court threw out the first verdict. This time, the state worked toward the same end but in another way.

Maude Earll was recalled to the stand to testify that she received letters from her brother Ward, had seen his handwriting when she sat next to him in school, and that she could recognize it. The defense attempted to block her testimony but was overruled. She swore that the writing on the sign was not in Ward's handwriting and the signature on it was not his. "He signed his name W. B. Earl, not Ward Earl," she said.[26]

Apparently in an attempt to reinforce the argument that Batson wrote the note left on Ward Earll's door, an Earll neighbor, N. L. Kelly, testified that he had passed Ward's place "three or four days before the bodies were discovered," and saw a note tacked to the door. Next, another neighbor, Henry Precht, said he went to the place three days after the bodies were found and that he found a piece of paper "about seven rods [about forty yards] southeast of the house," on which was written, "Gone, will be back, Sunday or Monday." Fred Earll then testified that Precht had given the paper to him, and that he had given it to the district attorney. "I know my brother's handwriting," Fred said. However, the newspaper reports do not say whether Fred said the handwriting on the note was or was not Ward's.[27]

The defense objected when the district attorney offered the paper as evidence, arguing that it was not found until four days after the discovery of the bodies, many people had been on the premises between the time the victims were found and when Precht found the paper, and the note was not connected to the case. Judge Miller allowed the note into evidence.[28]

The defense attorneys did score a few points when the state tried to introduce the gray vest allegedly found in the buggy left at the Downs stable. Deputy Horace Lyons, who recovered the vest and other items from the buggy, testified that the vest introduced in court this time was not the same one he had found in the buggy and was not the same one that had been put into evidence in the first trial.[29]

Clerk of court Gill told the court, "I know there was a vest introduced in evidence in the last trial, but I cannot state that this is the same one. The vest was put in the vault with the other documents, but we have been moving about a great deal, things have been open to the public and may have been misplaced. There was nothing on the vest by which I could identify it."[30]

It was 6 P.M. when the clerk finished his testimony, but before adjourning, the judge told Gill to conduct a search for the vest that night. However, when the clerk appeared as the first witness the next morning, he was not allowed to testify about the vest. After some haggling and the defense's formal objection to testimony about the vest on grounds that there was no certainty that any vest produced could be linked to the accused man, the judge ruled in Batson's favor, and according to the *Daily American*, "the vest question was laid on the shelf."[31] John Downs gave the same testimony he gave in the first trial, adding only that the buggy Batson allegedly rode into town remained in front of his stable for eleven days before Deputy Lyons came to retrieve items from it. Others testified to seeing Batson in Lake Charles on February 14, and a series of witnesses tied up some incidentals before the prosecution rested its case.[32]

Defense attorneys Overton and Sompayrac "retired for a few minutes [for] consultation" before calling their first witness, Herman Rock, a businessman who said Batson was not the man who tried to sell the mules on February 14. He said he was present that morning at Ryan's stables where the man who identified himself as Ward Earll first brought the stock to be sold. Rock testified that he "never saw [the] defendant until [he] saw him in [the] court room," that he "did not see him at the stable at that time," and that he did not recognize Batson as the man he saw at the stables.[33]

The final witness that morning was H. L. Reese, a streetcar driver who nearly collided with the man with the mules. "We stopped to avoid a crash and I saw the man [with the mules] and spoke to him. . . . Batson is not the man I met," Reese said. He testified that the man he spoke to that day had a short, stubby beard and a sandy mustache. He said he saw no scars on the face of the man he almost collided with.[34]

After a break for lunch, Missouri probate judge F. W. Coon took the stand. He had traveled eight hundred miles to testify as a character witness for Batson, who had been Coon's student when the judge taught in the public school. He said Batson's "character for peace and quiet is good," adding, "I have never been able to satisfy myself that Batson was guilty." Judge Coon brought with him a sworn statement by the sheriff who arrested Batson in Missouri stating that Batson had "demeaned himself in a quiet and gentlemanly manner" while in custody there.[35]

The defense then called Welsh newspaper writer George A. Bailey, who said a pair of bloody gloves alleged to have been Batson's actually belonged to one of the men who had helped move the bodies from Ward Earll's house.

"[I] went over to the house and saw the bodies," he said. "[They] were moved while I was there. . . . In moving the bodies, one of the men got a pair of gloves in the crowd to help. . . . After they were moved one glove was dropped at the corner of the house and the other near where the old man's body was found. . . . The blood about the bodies had dried; don't know if the blood on the gloves came from moving the bodies or not."[36]

That was it. The defense closed its case without calling Batson or any more witnesses, surprising practically everyone in the courtroom, including Ed Batson and his mother. As Underwood notes, "It had been thought that the defense had strong alibi witnesses in the wings, and that Batson would take the stand. No one was more surprised than Mrs. Payne, Batson's mother. When asked by a reporter what she thought of the sudden end of the defense case she did not at first realize that the case had closed. . . . Later she said she thought his defense lawyers had made a mistake by not putting him on the stand to tell his story, but 'they did what they thought best, and I am not blaming them.'"[37]

Indeed, during the preliminaries on the second day of the trial, the defense said it would call nine witnesses and made an issue of it when one of them, a Mrs. Olsen, was not present in court because of illness. According to press accounts, "The attorneys for the defense said that they could not go to trial unless they were assured that she would be able to testify when wanted, so Deputy Richard was detailed to obtain accurate information and in the meantime court took a recess. Attorney Sompayrac for the defense stated that [unless Mrs. Olsen's testimony was ensured] they would be obliged to ask for a continuance. Judge Miller directed the attorneys to make out their affidavit for a continuance and gave them thirty minutes to prepare it. When the time had expired, Mrs. Olsen was present in court, ending that phase of the case."[38] Despite the emphasis put on the importance of her testimony by defense lawyers, she was never called to the stand, nor was it ever revealed why her testimony was deemed so important at the beginning of the trial.

State prosecuting attorney A. R. Mitchell began his opening argument at 2:20 P.M. on the afternoon of Thursday, March 12, again showing the oratorical skill he demonstrated in the first trial. According to the *Weekly American*,

> He was eloquent and strong. He painted a lurid picture of the horrible crime, clothing it in well-chosen terms, and dwelling on the sight presented to Miss Maude Earl when she entered the chamber of death. . . . He also stated that while his attitude towards the prisoner was a neutral one, the evidence was such that the jury could not . . . return a verdict other than guilty, with capital punishment. He said that in his opinion, they could award either an acquittal or the death penalty, with no intermediary. . . . Dwelling on the [man] who had committed [the murders] . . . he said that, should an artist offer to paint him a picture of a murderer . . . [it would be] the face of A. E. Batson."
>
> Mr. Mitchell's argument was so forceful, so filled with selected verbiage and convincing terms, that the jury listened to him, breathless, and many spectators, at his reference to the young girl's impressions on seeing her dead mother, were moved to tears.[39]

His eloquence was such that it even withstood the distraction of some of the new courtroom's plaster falling on the head of juror John Abney as Mitchell made his argument.[40]

For the defense, Winston Overton "made no attempt at oratory," but made "a forceful argument" that if Ed Batson had wanted to rob the Earlls he could have done it while Ward Earll was in Welsh celebrating Mardi Gras rather than waiting for him to come home and kill him. He concluded by asking the jurors if they could live with the "horror" of hanging an innocent man.[41]

The second defense attorney, Paul Sompayrac, "made a passionate appeal to weigh the evidence fully [and] to disregard the horrible picture that had been drawn of the accused by Mr. Mitchell." He pointed out conflicting evidence and testimony and, as he did in the first trial, reminded the jury that the case against Ed Batson was entirely circumstantial. "The state of Louisiana shuns the death penalty," he said. "The most civilized nations are abolishing it. . . . Do not cast a further blot on Calcasieu by convicting on insufficient evidence."[42]

District Attorney Moore made the final argument for the prosecution, summing up the evidence and, according to the press, making a case both "forceful and convincing."[43]

At 5:20 P.M. the district attorney finished his remarks, and shortly after that Judge Miller began his all-important charge to the jury, using the same language he used in the first trial. He told the jurors they could also return a lesser verdict of manslaughter, which did not carry the death penalty, and said in part:

> The accused . . . is presumed innocent until his guilt is established by legal evidence beyond a reasonable doubt. . . . If you, the jury have a reasonable doubt of the guilt of the accused after you have carefully considered . . . all the evidence . . . he . . . is entitled to that doubt and you should acquit him. You are sole judges of the law and the evidence, and also the exclusive judges of the credibility of all witnesses and the weight to be given . . . to the testimony of each.
>
> But while you are the sole . . . judges of the law and the evidence, when you have found facts which you believe have been proven beyond a reasonable doubt you are morally bound to apply the law which has been given you by the court. You cannot rightfully exercise the . . . power of disregarding the instructions of the court upon the law any more than you can rightfully find a verdict opposed to the proof of the facts.
>
> Circumstantial evidence is legal evidence and a party accused may be convicted on circumstantial evidence alone. But . . . where a criminal charge is to be proved by circumstantial evidence, the proof ought to be not only consistent with the

> prisoner's guilt, but inconsistent with any other reasonable conclusion or hypothesis.
>
> Now, if you believe from the evidence beyond a reasonable doubt that [the] accused, A. E. Batson, killed . . . L. S. Earll, Mrs. L. S. Earll, Ward Earll, Fay Earl, John Earll and Lemuel Earll, or any one of them with premeditated design to kill . . . it will be your duty to find him . . . guilty as charged, in which event you may qualify your verdict by adding thereto, without capital punishment. A verdict with such a qualification in this case will consign the accused to life imprisonment in the state penitentiary at hard labor for life instead of suffering the death penalty upon the gallows.[44]

According to press reports, the jury voted unanimously on its first ballot that Ed Batson was guilty of murder but was evenly divided six to six on whether he should be hanged or sent to prison for life. "Four of the latter, however, changed their votes at once," according to the *Weekly American*, "and one more came over on the next ballot. The members refrained from discussing the case for some little time and when the next ballot was taken . . . they were all agreed."[45]

The jury returned at 8:30 P.M. with the verdict: guilty as charged. Ed Batson was unmoved. At first his mother seemed also to be, but then a minute later, according to a press account, "she was seen to quiver from head to toe." The report continued,

> She braced herself, sat upright, with her chin in her hand and remained in that position for several minutes. The courtroom was wrapped in silence. Suddenly Mrs. Payne fell back in her chair with a groan. Her face [was] of death-like paleness, her form became rigid, and she appeared dead. Sheriff Perkins and his deputies started towards her, but her condemned son, at her side, was the first to administer to her. He put his arm around her neck, opened her clothing at the throat and rubbed her hands in an effort to revive her.
>
> A cot was brought into the courtroom and the unfortunate woman laid upon it. Stimulants were administered and in a few

> minutes she revived. Her first words on regaining consciousness were: "Are we still in the courtroom?" Then she asked for her son. He had his arms around her neck. She pressed him to her heart. Their lips met. She wept aloud, saying, "My boy, oh my poor boy," all the time holding him close.
>
> A deputy touched Batson on the shoulder. He wanted to take him to the murderer's cage [jail cell]. The stricken woman pled with them and asked them not to separate her from her son. The condemned man looked at the officers in mute appeal. There were tears in his eyes.
>
> For the first time since his incarceration, the stolid Batson weakened. He leaned upon his hand. His face assumed an aged appearance. His eyes sank far back in his head, lines appeared around his mouth, dark circles were under his eyes, and his face twitched horribly in a supreme effort to refrain from weeping.[46]

A perversely curious crowd followed as Ed Batson, surrounded by a squad of deputies, was taken back to his cell, but Batson by then had "recovered his impenetrable composure." He bid the crowd a hearty good night from the door to the jail. When a reporter asked him if he had anything to say, he replied, "They have treated me mighty bad. I am innocent of the crime they have convicted me of." Then he stepped into his cell, and the door was closed behind him.[47]

19

Resignation

"Great crowds" flocked to the Calcasieu Parish jail on the day after Ed Batson's conviction. People climbed the stairs that wound around the gallows built inside the jail to file by Batson's cell and gawk at him.[1]

The steady flow of the curious did not seem to bother the prisoner, who told a newspaper reporter that he'd slept well the night after his conviction but he was worried about his mother. "He was told that she was better," the reporter for the *Lake Charles Weekly American* wrote. "He heaved a sigh of relief and seemed to be satisfied. He answered very promptly and good-humouredly a multitude of queries put to him by the curious throng outside the cage."[2]

He also made a statement for the press, reiterating his claims of innocence and giving again his account of how he traveled by train from Welsh to Missouri. "That talk about me having a disagreement with the Earls is all mistake," he said. "We were good friends. I might say, very good friends. They always treated me nicely and Mr. and Mrs. Earl treated me more like a son than a stranger. . . . I got anything I asked them for. The last time I saw them all, they were well and enjoying good health. We parted good friends with no hard feelings whatever."[3]

Reporters also visited a distraught Rachel Payne in her room at the Walker House where she was staying. "She was confined to her bed, and complained of pains in her head. She was asked to speak on the verdict, but the reference to the subject caused the tears to come to her eyes. She was completely unnerved, and had not yet recovered from the shock she had sustained."[4]

She said she had been taken unaware by the verdict:

> For Ed's sake, I had steeled myself and had myself under complete control, and would not have broken down, but . . . I felt so confident of Ed's acquittal that for a moment I forgot myself and the shock of the thing took me off my guard, and I weakened completely. . . . I think they have treated Ed very unjustly. . . . I do not want to criticize anyone, but I do think they gave my boy a bad brand of justice. I know he is innocent of that terrible crime, and some of these days they will discover the real murderer. If they had not inflicted the death penalty, but had sent him to prison for life, it would not have been so bad for we might some day ferret out the real criminal.[5]

Batson's mother said she would go back to Missouri and "enlist the aid of [her] friends in an effort to get Governor Dockery, of Missouri, to use his influence with the governor of Louisiana to have the sentence at least commuted to life imprisonment."[6]

Batson's defense attorneys had the same idea. They released a statement saying they would not appeal the verdict because they were convinced "the record contains no reversible error. . . . . Our connection with the Batson case is now at an end."[7] However, they did submit the trial records to the Louisiana Board of Pardons suggesting that Batson's punishment of hanging was too harsh for a man sentenced with only circumstantial evidence of his guilt.

Judge Coon, who had traveled from Missouri to testify in Batson's behalf and to watch the trial, shared the opinion of Batson's lawyers, Overton and Sompayrac. He had suggested before the trial that it would be hard for a defendant to get fair treatment when "charged with so grave a crime, with such a chain of circumstantial evidence as the State claims to have against him, eight hundred miles from home, without friends or money." Since the evidence was wholly circumstantial, "the people should carefully weigh the matter, and the defendant should have ample time to make a complete defense, which cannot always be done in a few days or weeks in such a case," he said.[8]

But after having watched the trial, the Missouri judge told the press he was "satisfied with the fairness with which Batson has been dealt" and that Batson "has had as fair and impartial [a] trial as he could have secured in his own state, and [he had] nothing but praise for [attorneys] Sompayrac and Overton in [their] untiring efforts in Batson's behalf." Judge Coon continued, "I came to Louisiana with my mind unsatisfied as to his guilt or innocence and was in hopes that he would be able to establish his innocence. However, under the circumstances there was but one of two things for the jury to do—either find him guilty as charged or acquit him. The evidence against the boy was very strong . . . and the verdict is in accordance with it. I have no one to criticize or censure."[9]

It is a bit curious that neither the sheriff who arrested Batson in Missouri nor the one who brought him back to Louisiana testified at either of the trials. When he was bringing the prisoner back from Missouri, Sheriff Perkins told the press that Ed Batson certainly didn't look like a murderer. Did prosecutors not put Perkins on the stand because he would have said the same things under oath, in effect, becoming a minor character witness for Batson?

Ed Batson said he had been "anxious" to take the stand in his own behalf, as he had in the first trial, but his lawyers convinced him not to testify. He said if he had testified, his testimony would have been the story he told all along.

> I had no words or any quarrel with [Ward Earll] and told him that I was going home. He paid me $11.25, giving me two five-dollar bills, four quarters, and the rest in nickels and small change. The two boys Fay and Lemuel came up in a wagon on their way to school before I left, and between nine and ten o'clock I left Ward Earl's house and walked out on the railroad track and then along the track to Welsh. The hands were plowing in old man Earl's field when I passed. . . . When I went to work for the Earls, I was told that they were hard people to get

> along with, but I did not find them so. They treated me well, paid me every cent they owed me and I had no cause whatsoever to complain.
>
> I might have gone to the Bell store and bought a box of cartridges the day Miss Maud and the other young lady say I did, for I often went there and bought cartridges. I may have also asked for BB shells, for I often bought that kind there, using them for shooting brant in the prairie. Such large shot are generally used for this purpose as the brant are wild and they have to be shot at long range for a shotgun.[10]
>
> As for stealing the mules, why that it is out of the question. If I did want to steal them I would not need to kill anybody. A dozen times Ward Earll . . . went away and left me in charge of the animals for two or three weeks at a time. I could have run the stock off easily at almost any time if I had wanted to.[11]

Batson was finally sentenced to death a week after the end of his trial, and according to the *Daily American*, the courtroom scenes from the first and second sentencings were far different. "The first time he listened to the judge's dread pronouncement . . . the noted prisoner faced the court with the assurance that an appeal would be made . . . with the strong possibility of reversal," the newspaper reported on March 19, 1903. "Today he heard the sentence of death with no appeal, no legal delays to intervene and with nothing but the faint hope of official clemency standing between him and the gallows." Batson's demeanor at the sentencing showed he "appreciated the gravity of the situation. . . . His face was flushed, his eyes bright with excitement and his mien serious."[12]

The judge was also more subdued. Unlike at the first hearing, when Judge Miller ordered Batson to hang until he was "dead, dead, dead," this time, he "hurried over" the sentence, "speaking almost inaudibly."[13]

Once again, "Batson listened without a quiver, inclined his head respectfully at the end, and walked calmly back to his seat."[14]

20

Enter Dobson

Charles M. Dobson, who identified himself as a former correspondent for the Associated Press, appeared on the scene in time to witness Ed Batson's second trial, and not quite three months later published a little book titled *Guilty? Side Lights on the Batson Case.*

A friend of the defense attorneys, Dobson said he wrote the book solely to present "this celebrated affair to the general public" and that he tried to present the facts and evidence of the case "devoid of bias."[1] Nonetheless, he created a scenario in which two men, whom he identifies only as "number one" and "number two," tracked the Earlls for twenty years because of some old wrong done to them or their family before the Earlls moved to Louisiana. These two men, Dobson contended, collaborated in stalking and murdering the family in revenge for this long-ago deed.[2]

Dobson begins his tale on the night of February 8, 1902, four days before the Earll murder:

> The west bound Southern Pacific train from New Orleans to Houston had [reached] Lake Charles about seven in the evening, and among a number of the passengers that alighted were two men who had boarded the train at New Orleans. For a portion of the way these men occupied different coaches, but occasionally one of them, a man about forty-seven years of age, mustached, dark complexion, slightly above the medium height, and dressed in the neutral way which does not bespeak occupation, went forward in the train and stooped down while resting his hand on the back of the seat occupied by the second man,

Journalist Charles Dobson. Photo reproduced from Charles Dobson, *Guilty? Side Lights on the Batson Case* (New Orleans, 1903), left-hand page, on other side of title page.

> saying a few words which could not be overheard by the other passengers. The movements of the first man would have indicated to a close observer that number one was explaining to the seated passenger the location of various land marks. When left alone for a space of over an hour, it was observed that number two frequently consulted the map contained in the time-folder as if . . . to locate the whereabouts of the train.[3]

In Dobson's account the seated passenger, number two, rode on the right side of the train until it reached Crowley, just east of Welsh, when he changed to the left side, revealing to anyone who looked that he had a scar on the left side of his face.[4]

The train was just pulling out of Welsh, Dobson wrote, "when the first man . . . came swiftly into the car from the rear and placing his hand on number two's shoulder, said in

SIXTH EDITION

GUILTY?

SIDE LIGHTS ON

THE BATSON CASE

A RECRUDESCENSE OF THE MURDER OF THE EARLL FAMILY IN LOUISIANA, 1902

—BY—

CHARLES DOBSON, Ph. D.

JUNE, 1903

The L. Graham Company, Ltd., New Orleans

COPYRIGHT—All Rights Reserved

Title page of Dobson's book. Image reproduced from Charles Dobson, *Guilty? Side Lights on the Batson Case* (New Orleans, 1903), no page number.

a low voice, 'Here! Here!! About two miles and you will see the lights!' and then started for the car ahead. He had gone but half the length of the car when he returned to the seat occupied by number two, and in a low tone said: 'We slow up at Iowa Crossing. The stop after that will be the coal-chute at Lake Charles. Get off there. Do not wait to go to the depot.'"[5]

The train did not stop for coal at the side track on the outskirts of town, but went into Lake Charles and stopped near the town's commercial district. The two men left the train separately. Number one led the way, and number two trailed fifty yards behind as they walked to the Traveler's Rest, a hotel "which in point of fact more resembled a private residence." They registered under the names of H. H. George and E. S. John of Madison, Iowa.[6]

About 9 o'clock on the same night, Dobson said, the man with the scar came downstairs and paid a week's board in advance. The writer described the scarred man as "lighter in weight than his companion, weighing probably one hundred and sixty-five pounds, about five feet eleven inches in height, with blue eyes and fresh complexion."[7]

> Several hours [later] . . . these two men were closeted together in their room. They appeared to be interested in the perusal of a number of documents and photographs which "number one" had in his possession. One photograph in particular was selected and was standing on the table resting against a glass filled with water. From amongst a number of documents . . . "number one" selected a printed document . . . [that] appeared to be some form of an insurance policy, containing an identification of apparently [the person in] the photograph resting against the glass, since the two frequently compared the photograph and the identification or description.[8]

Dobson claims that on the following morning the two men left the hotel separately but met at the Lake City Saloon where they spent the day watching poker games and checking on the horse-racing results sent by telegraph from the New Orleans racetrack. On the night of February 10 they left Lake Charles together on the eastbound train, getting off at Welsh, where they took a room at the Signal Hotel.[9]

On the morning of February 11, according to Dobson, the man with the scar hired a buggy and a driver, and was driven to a farm near Welsh. From there he walked across rice fields to the Earll farm, where "on seeing the visitor, it was clear that [L. S. Earll] recognized him, and the hesitancy on the part of Mr. Earll indicated considerable confusion and astonishment. After looking at the visitor fully ten seconds without speaking, the old man held up one hand, his arm outstretched, and said a single word, 'wait,' and at the top of his voice yelled, 'Batson, hitch up. I am going to Welsh.'"[10]

At no point in his narrative does Dobson indicate how he became privy to what went on behind closed doors or to the conversations among the several men involved in the affair. During this passage he tells the reader that the discussion between L. S. Earll and number two "could only be gleaned from the remarks of Mr. Earll."[11]

According to Dobson,

> Earll reportedly told number two, Yes, he would make all the reparation he possibly could. He had not yet the money for his rice. He did not know exactly when he would receive the money, but he could probably get a few hundred dollars that day or the next. He had no objection to parting with his stock. . . . As they were approaching the outskirts of [Welsh], the man with the scar placed his hands on the lines and said: "Stop here. I will be out tomorrow, and you will make good then. I will take that stock, and damn you! I never want to see or hear of you again." Mr. Earll then turned the buggy to the west and drove toward the Earll homestead. The visitor walked into Welsh, and reported the result of the visit to number one, who received it with indifference and without comment.[12]

The following morning, February 12, "number two" walked from Welsh to the Earll homestead "and there received money," according to Dobson's account. On leaving the house the stranger met Batson, the hired man, and observed that Batson had a scar on his face similar to the scar on his own.[13] Charles Dobson professed to believe that the mysterious scarred man, number two, was the man witnesses saw leading the Earll stock to Lake Charles and that look-alike Ed Batson was already riding the rails on his way home to his mother, as he claimed from the beginning.

If number two was not simply a figment of Dobson's imagination, his presence would explain one discrepancy in the account given by the principal witness, John Downs. In the first newspaper story after the crime, Downs said the man who came to his stable with Ward Earll's stock had a scar on the left side of his face, as did Dobson's number two.[14] Batson's scar was on the right side of his face. Nonetheless, Downs used that "unmistakable" mark to identify Batson from newspaper photographs and in person.[15]

According to Dobson: "Mr. [L. S.] Earll returned to the house, and calling Batson, the hired man, told him that his son, Ward Earll, required his services no longer, to which Batson replied that he was sorry, but that as he had received a letter from his mother . . . asking him to come home, 'It suited him very well.' . . . After this, the old man looked at [Batson] and said, 'do you know that man who was here just now? It is funny, but you look alike, and if it were not for the difference in your ages, I should take you for brothers.'"[16]

Again, it is not clear how the seemingly omnipresent Dobson overheard this conversation, nor how he could have recreated it with L. S. Earll being dead and the strangers No. 1 and No. 2 long gone and never heard from again. Batson himself is not quoted in Dobson's text, and there is no indication that the two ever spoke to each other.

According to Dobson's account, a man with a scar on the left side of his face was seen on the road west of Welsh at 3:15 P.M. on February 13, driving a buggy that was hitched with four mules and two horses. "About one mile before this," Dobson continues, "at precisely 2:55 he had left the man . . . known as 'number one.' . . . The same night this . . . (number one) was seen on the west-bound Southern Pacific Express. He stood on the rear platform of the train as it . . . left Iowa junction when the brakeman came through the door. 'Land-looking?' he [the brakeman] remarked. 'No,' was the brusque reply. 'Sent some stock ahead of me, thought I might see them.'"[17]

In Dobson's version, number two, the scarred man with the Earll stock, stopped at a barroom in Iowa after seven o'clock on the night of February 13, ordered a pint of whiskey, and asked if there was someplace where he could stay the night. The bartender referred him to Funk's store, where he was told that a Mr. Findlay sometimes put up "traveling men." The man arrived at Findlay's about 7:30 P.M. and paid $2.50 to spend the night in Findlay's barn.[18]

"Without much ado the stranger threw himself into the hay—took a long pull at his whiskey bottle, and after sharing his contents with [a black man also sleeping in the barn], soon fell asleep," Dobson continues. "He did not sleep very well. Again and again the negro was awakened by some loud exclamation of the sleeping man, evidently the result of a heavy dream re-enacting some lively and disagreeable reflection of the past. It was a night of terror for the superstitious [black man], who kept tossing on his bed of hay, anxiously awaiting the breaking of dawn."[19]

At full daylight the man with a scar on the left side of his face left Iowa and got to Lake Charles nearly at noon on February 14, Dobson recounts. After almost colliding with a "magnificent 'electric' mule car," as he describes a Lake Charles trolley, the man found his way to Ed Ryan's stable, where he haggled for two hours over the price of stock. Reaching no bargain, he then went to John Downs's stable to try his luck, getting there about three thirty in the afternoon. The man with the scar identified himself as Ward Earll.[20]

Dobson continues:

> The lights of the stores on Ryan Street, the main thoroughfare of Lake Charles, burned brightly on the night of February 14th, 1902—groups of men lounged here and there on the east side of the street. The Lake City Saloon, the resort of the better drinking and sporting element, was crowded and the huge mirrors reflected a line of figures and faces which were remarkable to a degree for variety of stature, intelligence and headgear. Lumbermen, bank employees, rice men, gamblers, city officials, petty politicians and drummers were indulging in the inevitable . . . cocktail. Everyone seemed to know everyone else, and when occasionally a man strayed through the door and became merged in the motley crush, one of those present would know him, and [even though] they may have met only once before, the last comer would be introduced to all hands, which ceremony was the signal for "another ball."[21]

The man known as number one sat at a table a little apart from the crowd, an untouched plate of oysters before him. Just behind him was a door with a glass window, "at which there suddenly appeared a white face pressed closely against the glass. The white face had a scar on its left side. Number two opened the door and approached the preoccupied number one. The man with the scar was dressed in a rubber coat, gum boots, and a soft white hat."[22]

> As the newcomer touched him on the shoulder, [number one] leaped to his feet with a muttered blasphemous exclamation, and a quick movement of his right hand towards his right rear pocket. On recognizing the new arrival he sat down again quickly as if in a state of semi-collapse, while the other looked on in astonishment. . . . Without further conversation, they left the room by the back door through which the face had been seen, and passing through the alley-way leading to Bilbo Street, turning to the south . . . and ascended the west verandah of the Howard House [hotel], where they entered together, going direct to the writing room in the rear of the office. When they had seated themselves . . . the man with the scar ejaculated, "Now then, what about it? What did you do?" The whole reply could not be heard, but the tail end . . . was audible to the extent of "The whole lot. There is not one left." At this, [number two] started to his feet; leaning over, caught "number one" by the lapel of his coat, and pulling towards him, with his face not more than an inch away, and staring him straight in the eyes, said in an excited tone, "You do not mean it?" . . . "Yes, I do mean it," number one replied. "It could not be helped. That makes eight."
>
> "Let me tell you," number two said, "I am through with this. I did not think you would go so far. It was totally unnecessary, and you have got me mixed up in this affair to an extent far beyond my calculation. I shall leave at once. So far as the stock is concerned, it can remain where it is. I will not go back to get the money, and, besides, neither your life or mine is worth a minute's purchase twelve hours from now. That liveryman telephoned Daniels today and he is expected on the evening train."[23]

After that conversation, the two men agreed to leave Lake Charles immediately. Number one took an eastbound train from Lake Charles to New Orleans, while number two walked five miles to the west from Lake Charles to the town of Sulphur, stayed overnight there at the Hotel Imperial, and got aboard a westbound train for Houston the next day. Unfortunately, neither number one nor number two were ever seen or heard from again (nor were they particularly sought after by authorities).

Dobson's story, even if unlikely, did create an alternative scenario just plausible enough for the circumstantial evidence against Batson to also point to another man. But, as Underwood noted, "It cannot be determined from the available record whether the defense actually had witnesses to back up Dobson's theories. It cannot be said with any certainty which threads of his elaborate mosaic were based on fact and which were pure invention."[24]

Nonetheless, Underwood says, although much of Dobson's so-called evidence would be "inadmissible and probably nonexistent," it was convincing enough that "there are still people living . . . around Welsh who accept his version of the crime as fact and believe that Batson was the innocent victim of a conspiracy."[25]

21

Indignation and False Hope

On July 29, 1903, the *New Orleans Picayune*'s front-page headline announced: "Lake Charles Thrown into a Wild Ferment." Townspeople learned that day that Louisiana's pardon board, consisting of three members—attorney general Walter Guion, lieutenant governor Albert Estopinal, and Judge Miller—had issued an opinion that Batson's sentence should be changed to life imprisonment.[1]

The board's action was not wholly unexpected. The *Lake Charles Daily American* reported in May that "A. E. Batson will not be hanged during the next eight weeks, and an application has been made for the commutation of his sentence which may result in his not being hanged at all. . . . A gentleman . . . who knows the conditions better perhaps than any other man, said he believed that there had been a change in sentiment among the people of Lake Charles to the extent that they would not like to see the man hanged, because of the large element of circumstantial evidence."[2] The unnamed gentleman apparently misread the public mind.

Judge Miller was not present when the other two members concluded that the circumstantial evidence offered in the case was strong enough to convict Batson of stealing stock but was not strong enough to convict him of murder. Miller, who recommended keeping the death penalty, said he had to be in court in Lake Charles at the time the others decided to meet in New Orleans, and he was "greatly astonished" when he heard what the other two members of the pardon board had decided.[3] Apparently the people of Lake Charles and Welsh reacted with the same dismay. Citizens of Lake Charles called a mass meeting to denounce the pardon board decision. "At first incredulity sat upon every face, and the words, 'No, impossible,' were heard on every side," the *Daily American* reported, "and then indignation—deep and strong—broke loose, mingled with words of praise for Judge Miller, who refused to concur with the Board's action." According to the newspaper, people in Welsh were "dumbfounded," and "expressions of indignation and disgust are heard" throughout the town.[4] The *Welsh Rice Belt Journal* reported,

> During the fervor of excitement some even boldly asserted that such action on the part of those in whose hand the fate of a twice convicted murderer had been entrusted was an incentive to mob law. . . . It rests with the governor now as to whether he will act on the recommendation of the board. If he pigeon-holes the recommendation, Batson will hang at the scheduled time. If he grants the commutation, Batson will not hang, legally, and if he gets to the penitentiary he stands a good chance of liberty at the end of fifteen years. . . . So the man twice convicted of a sextuple murder stands a good chance of not only saving his neck, but also of walking out into the world a free man. And all because he was wise enough to keep his mouth shut and had the coolness and the bravado to keep a stiff upper lip under the most trying of circumstances. There were many who were strong in the belief of the guilt of Batson, and they believed that his nerve would desert him when he saw the gallows in front of him, and then he would tell the story of his horrible crime.[5]

Lake Charles resident M. K. Shaddock suggested at the mass meeting that the two pardon board members had been misguided in reaching their decision by reading Charles Dobson's book.[6] Attorney General Guion (no apparent relation to state attorney Louis Guion who argued the case at both trials) gave the board's reasons for the commutation after the second trial. They included consideration of a number of "numerously signed" petitions asking the board to commute the sentence, including one signed by John Downs, "the witness who swore to the identification of Batson as the person

Attorney General Walter Guion. *Photo courtesy of LOUISiana Digital Library,* http://louisdl.louislibraries.org/.

found in possession of the live stock of Ward Earll . . . [but] who, with others [said] the sentence was based entirely on circumstantial evidence, not of a nature sufficient to justify the verdict and the sentence."[7]

Further, Attorney General Guion said, "We believe that we are justified in the statement that Batson was not identified by any one as the person who had left the Earl gun with a gunsmith for repairs, nor was any evidence introduced that was, in our opinion, sufficient to connect him with the person who left the watch in the hands of the jeweler in Lake Charles."[8]

Most important, Guion said, "We believe we are justified in stating that the only identification of Batson was by the witness Downs and several others, who testified that he was the man in possession of the live stock . . . although there were other witnesses who testified he was not the man. . . . A street car driver says that he nearly ran into the stock, and he is sure the man driving [the stock] was not Batson."[9]

Lieutenant Governor Albert Estopinal.
Photo courtesy of LOUISiana Digital Library, http://louisdl.louislibraries.org/.

The two pardon board members agreed that even if the man with the stock was Batson, that fact alone was not conclusive evidence that he killed six members of the Earll family for the mules and horses. "It might have been sufficient, coupled with other facts . . . to warrant his conviction for larceny, but we hardly felt warranted in extending the presumption [of guilt] any further. The law covers that point. Possession of personal property, such as a man's watch that he was known to have . . . might justify the presumption of murder but in the case of live stock, it is not altogether improbable that a man might be murdered in his home and another man steal his stock without any collusion with the murderer."[10] The two board members who voted for commutation admitted, however, that they were forced to make their decision on the basis of interviews with witnesses, since no transcript had been kept of Batson's trial.[11]

Newspaper reporters gathered at the sheriff's office and went with him to Batson's cell, where Sheriff Perkins handed the condemned man a copy of the Houston paper that reported the commutation recommendation. "Batson read the item in absolute silence, and held the paper with a hand that was absolutely steady," the *Picayune* reported. "After a moment the Picayune reporter said that the same news had been received from New Orleans, and when Batson was asked if he had heard the news [already], . . . he replied that Mr. Overton . . . had called to tell him that [they had taken action on the recommendation]." Overton had not been able to gain access to the jail but "shouted to him from the outside" causing "the inmates . . . [to] burst into a cheer when they heard it."[12]

According to the *Daily American*, "On being asked if he had anything to say, [Batson] replied that he had nothing to give out, and smilingly referred to the rainy weather. Questioned as to whether he had ever given up hopes of having his sentence commuted, he said, with a little grin [that he had not] . . . and that he knew it was only a question of time when the news would be brought to him of this fact."[13] Batson said "the boys confined in the cages west of him were so glad to hear the news that they gave vent to their feelings very strongly and their voices were heard a block away."[14]

Batson asked the sheriff to send a telegram to his sister in Missouri, which read: "Sentence commuted. Let mother know." Then, according to the report, "Never losing his nerve, always with a twinkle in his eyes, he wished his audience good morning, and when they turned to go, seated himself on his couch [cot], and resumed reading his novel, 'The Lost Bride.'"[15]

Overton told reporters later that he thought the governor would abide by the recommendation. Both the lieutenant governor and attorney general were political allies of the governor and had run with him on the Democratic State Ticket in 1900.

The other defense attorney, Paul Sompayrac, said he believed all along the board would commute the sentence.[16] But the board's recommendation was not binding on the governor, and Judge Miller and the townspeople of Lake Charles made sure that Governor Heard understood their dismay.

Several hundred of the "coolest and most conservative people" of Calcasieu Parish gathered at the courthouse on the evening of the announcement "to protest against the action . . . and to urge upon the Governor the vast importance of refusing to interfere with the execution of the man who is recognized by all who know the evidence in the case as the most dastardly murderer who has yet been before the courts of the parish," the *New Orleans Picayune* noted.[17]

The *Picayune* writer called the crowd "thoroughly representative," saying it included merchants, city officials, bank representatives, ministers, and others from "every walk of life." The meeting, the reporter wrote, was "harmonious," with "nothing being said or done that could have been classed as passionate or hasty."[18] Lake Charles alderman E. L. Crosby, chairman of the protest meeting, said he was there "simply as a law-abiding citizen who wished to see the laws of the land upheld and a criminal dealt with in a lawful manner. He stated that nothing was further from his mind or the minds of any who came to participate in that meeting than thoughts of violence, and that only a fear of what such a meeting unskillfully guided might lead to cause[d] him to hesitate to take the position he had been asked to take."[19]

A committee was appointed to draft a resolution to the governor, which said in part:

> Whereas, the law-abiding citizens of Calcasieu Parish have kept faith with Governor Heard, in his promise to the governor of Missouri that Batson should have a fair and impartial trial; and, whereas, said Batson has had two fair and impartial trials by the best people of our parish composing the two juries, and has been twice convicted and sentenced to expiate upon the gallows the foul and infamous crimes committed by him.
>
> Now, therefore, resolved, That we the citizens of Calcasieu Parish, in mass meeting assembled, do hereby express our solemn protest against the said recommendation of the lieutenant governor and attorney general, as members of the board of pardons.
>
> Resolved, That we do earnestly request His Excellency, the Governor of the State of Louisiana, not to defeat the ends of justice, but to assist the law-abiding people of this parish by declining to set aside the verdict of two juries.[20]

Writing and adoption of the resolution took ninety minutes, then "the people retired to their homes, feeling as if they had done their duty towards humanity."[21]

Opinion was divided outside Calcasieu Parish. In Alexandria, the central Louisiana town where Sheriff Perkins feared on the trip back from Missouri that Batson would be hanged in the rail yard, a *Louisiana Democrat* editorial supported the pardon board. "We believe it has been the uniform custom of our Governor since the establishing of the pardoning board . . . [in] 1879 to [follow] the recommendations of the board . . . without expressing any opinion on the correctness of the verdict of the jury." Since this verdict was "rendered upon circumstantial evidence alone, it occurs to us that it would be wise [for] Governor Heard . . . to follow the precedent of his predecessors and commute the sentence as recommended."[22]

The *Daily American* reported from the south Louisiana sugarcane center of Donaldsonville that "people throughout the state feel humiliated at the manner in which the 'citizens' of Lake Charles are carrying on. They held a mass meeting . . . and their actions and resolutions . . . show clearly that they are bent on mischief. It is hoped that Gov. Heard will not allow himself to be bluffed by a few blood-thirsty people who are crying out like a frenzied mob for the life of Batson."[23]

The *Daily American* also reported that in Lafayette, midway between New Orleans and Lake Charles, editors of the *Gazette* made the following point: "A number of Louisiana papers are not satisfied with the verdict in the Batson case and are advocating a commutation of the sentence. Without wishing to express any opinion as to the guilt or innocence of Batson it strikes us that the courts of Calcasieu are more competent to try criminal cases in that parish than newspapers located in different sections of the state."[24]

The editorial writer for the *Daily American* raised the specter of a "Judge Lynch" (meaning a lynching mob) and said the blame would lie at the feet of the attorney general if such a situation occurred.

> Whatever the governor's decision, the people of Calcasieu have done their full duty and are not to blame for the outcome. They

> have given the courts full swing at the case which exerted the horror of the country; they have repressed the mob law spirit; they have given the prisoner the best of legal advice; they were patient when the first trial was overturned on a mere technicality and have given the accused a second fair and unprejudiced trial. If the governor sees fit to follow the advice of the state pardon board, The American hopes and believes that the decision will be soberly acquiesced in. If the miscarriage of justice gives Judge Lynch a wider field of action; if lawless people take courage from Batson's escape to perpetrate like outrages; if extremes therefore conclude to settle matters so that pardon boards and sentimentalists will be barred from intervening, the responsibility will rest upon the state's officers. In the attorney general's purview, Batson's guilt is in doubt for two reasons: (1) Because the jury convicted him and therefore was probably prejudiced; (2) Because Downs . . . felt tenderhearted enough to sign a petition on his behalf and therefore deemed him innocent. Mr. Downs will probably be surprised to know that he is a better judge of the law and the evidence than the court and the jury.[25]

Before making his final decision, the governor met privately with Judge Miller to review the evidence and hear the judge's impressions of Batson's demeanor. The judge convinced the governor of Batson's guilt. "I presided at both Batson trials," Judge Miller said. "Two separate juries found him guilty as charged. . . . I had plenty of time to observe the actions of the defendant in the courtroom and I am deeply convinced the man is guilty."[26]

In one of the few instances that Fred Earll was mentioned during both trials, his comment at the time of the commutation recommendation may have had as much influence on the governor as any of the legal arguments. "I do not believe Governor Heard will commute the sentence," the only surviving Earll son said, "but if he does, Batson will not get out of Lake Charles alive. I know of three or four hundred men who will not stand for it."[27]

There was also some legal maneuvering having to do with technicalities in the way in which Batson had been sentenced, but their effect was only to dot the i's and cross the t's rather than seriously challenge the sentence. In the end Ed Batson's fate was in the hands of Governor Heard, who decreed: "Batson must die."[28]

Had the pardon board's recommendation been accepted, Ed Batson would have been sentenced to life in prison, and under Act 112 of the 1890 Louisiana State Legislature, he would have been eligible for parole in fifteen years.[29] That is, if he made it to prison. The editors of the Princeton, Missouri, newspaper had their doubts about that, reporting on August 13: "There is little doubt but that if the governor had commuted the sentence Batson would have been mobbed before he could have been placed in the penitentiary, as such seemed to be the sentiment of the people of Lake Charles and Welsh."[30]

22

Last Chance

If Ed Batson faced his impending death with equanimity—perhaps bolstered by an unshakeable belief that his sentence would ultimately be commuted—the final weeks of his life were agonizing for his mother as she fought to the last to save her son from the gallows. In the days before the execution one last glimmer of hope remained, one last straw to clutch, but it too came to naught.

Rachel Payne was heartbroken when she saw her son on the evening of Thursday, August 13, the day before he was scheduled to die. By then both of them knew that only a miracle would save him, and neither of them believed in miracles. Mrs. Payne had gone to Baton Rouge where she spent an hour and a half pleading with Governor Heard, "using every argument and every plea that a mother could advance."[1] A rebirth of hope emerged when a bit of new evidence from two witnesses was found, but despite high expectations by the accused and his attorneys, the governor did not believe the additional evidence changed anything.[2]

Even though they declared after the second trial that their involvement with him was over, the defense attorneys also went to Baton Rouge on the evening of August 12 to plead their client's case once more with the governor and to present as evidence new affidavits given by "Mesdames Farris and Frazier" of Lake Charles testifying that Batson was not the man who tried to sell Ward Earll's horses in Lake Charles on February 14, 1902.[3]

The *Lake Charles Daily American* reported, "The . . . evidence upon which a reprieve will be asked . . . consists of affidavits from two women who reside in the northeast part of town who claim to have seen the man with the stock on that fateful day in February 1902. They claim that he was trying to sell the stock to an Italian storekeeper and that the man was not Batson, being a different looking man altogether."[4] According to the *New Orleans Picayune*, the two women went to the jail with Batson's mother to get a look at him and said he was not the man they saw that day trying to sell stock.[5]

"With our intimate acquaintance with the Batson case we believe that if the existence of this evidence had been known to us in time we could have presented it to [the] jury with much force. . . . it would have changed the character of the case," Sompayrac said. The governor, however, said he did not "consider that what was presented was material sufficient to the issue to change [his] decision to not interfere with the process of law."[6]

Governor Heard, a native of Union Parish in north Louisiana, was probably swayed as much by the politics of the situation as by the legalities. The former Louisiana legislator was very much aware that the sheriff, judge, and district attorney—the three most powerful politicians in Calcasieu Parish—not to mention a preponderance of the citizens of southwest Louisiana—were convinced that Ed Batson was guilty and that the death sentence was appropriate.[7]

Attorney Sompayrac, accompanied by a *New Orleans Picayune* reporter, brought the word to Ed Batson, who was expecting good news. When Batson saw his attorney coming toward his cell, he jumped up from his cot "with considerable vivacity and met his legal advisor at the . . . door to his cell with a hearty, 'How do you do, Mr. Sompayrac?'" When the lawyer said he had news from Baton Rouge, "Batson's face lit up rather expectantly."[8] The prisoner knew that a petition "from very influential sources in Missouri" had been sent to Governor Heard "and knew that the governor had granted his faithful mother an interview." Since he was "naturally a hopeful, determined, nervy sort of man," he "showed that he was glad to meet his attorney with news from the Governor."[9]

But, instead, his attorney told him, "The governor has refused to sign the commutation of sentence and you are doomed to hang." The attorney read a telegram from the governor's office, and then told his client, "Batson, if you are guilty of this crime . . . ask the forgiveness of God, and pray that your soul may be saved." Ed Batson hung his head but did not say a word.[10]

After he received the bad news, "the much talked of nerve of the criminal weakened slightly," according to the *Picayune*. "His countenance fell. He drew close to the man who had defended him and advised him through two celebrated trials. His face grew red and a tear trickled down his cheek as he looked mutely into the eyes of his attorney."[11]

Sompayrac asked Batson to undertake his ordeal like a man, and Batson "nodded his head in the affirmative," according to the press. "Mr. Sompayrac," he said, "you and Mr. Overton have done everything in your power for me, and I want to thank you, and say that I am perfectly satisfied." His lawyer said, "As this is the last time I will ever see you, I want to say good-bye. Good-bye, Batson, and may you rest in peace."[12] Ed Batson lay down on his cot, and his attorney and the newspaper reporter left without saying another word.[13]

The two women who had stirred up the last hope did not testify in either of Batson's trials, but gave their affidavits on Wednesday, August 10. Batson's mother also took the documents to Judge Miller, asking him to look at them and to issue a reprieve for her son. The judge, like the governor, did not consider the affidavits sufficient to reopen the case. Finally, according to the *Weekly American*, Mrs. Payne told Miller, "Judge, you have a son and he some day might be where my boy is." The judge replied, "It is possible, Mrs. Payne, and in such an event it is likely that I would be doing as you are—trying to delay his death, and save him from his fate in any way possible. You are doing a mother's part as you should, but a reprieve for a few days or weeks would only prolong the suspense and inflict on you anew the agony you are now undergoing. I sympathize with you, but I must perform my duty as I see it."[14]

After Ed Batson was hanged, Judge Miller told the *Picayune* that the trial had imposed "a most unpleasant duty upon him and one which he was loath to perform." But, he said, he did not see how a jury could reach any verdict other than guilty, and the verdict made it necessary for him to impose the death penalty. "Believing as [I] did fully in Batson's guilt," he said, "[I] could not do otherwise than differ with the two other members of the Board of Pardon."[15]

Governor Heard left "for a week's sojourn" on the Mississippi gulf coast before meeting with the grieving mother, saying he had spent a good part of the week weighing her son's fate. He told her "how he had carefully gone over all the papers in the case, and admitted that at one time he was inclined to harbor a doubt of [Batson's] guilt, but the interview with Judge Miller . . . removed all doubt and he had no recourse but to allow the law to take its course."[16]

According to the *Picayune*, "Mrs. Payne, though greatly disappointed, bore the ordeal bravely. She indulged in no violent demonstrations. Her grief was deep, but she suppressed her emotions."[17] However, the Welsh newspaper reported, "She spent only a short while in the governor's office, but the few officers of the executive department who were present at the time of the interview declared they hope never again to witness such bereavement as was expressed . . . [by] the grief-stricken mother when given to understand by the governor that she had best return to Lake Charles and spend the remaining days with her unfortunate son."[18]

The newspaper in Rachel Payne's hometown reported, "The action of the governor in not following the recommendation of the board of pardons is unprecedented,"[19]

As he contemplated his ordeal of the past year, Ed Batson told reporters, "I have the most noble mother in the world; she has worked and worked to do something for me since my incarceration. . . . She has not left anything undone which she thought or had the least idea would be of any benefit to her boy. . . . Others may forsake me, but my mother will not."[20]

As he spoke, three men, Dave Lyons, Bud Coley, and Tate Perkins, worked to finish the scaffold and gallows only three feet away from the door of his cell. During a good part of the morning the condemned prisoner leaned against the bars of his cell "and watched every piece of work done," sometimes joking with the workers, never saying a word "to make them believe he regretted being the one for which it was being erected."[21]

Two days before his scheduled execution, Batson said he had been slandered by a suggestion in the press that he was losing his nerve. On August 12, Batson told a *Daily American* reporter, "'They put that thing up there,'. . . indicating with a wave of his hand, the noose dangling within a few feet of him 'thinking that it would make me loose [*sic*] my nerve; but it doesn't affect me at all.'"[22]

23

No Escape, No Reprieve

According to some tantalizing stories, Ed Batson may have contemplated—even tried—escaping from the Calcasieu Parish jail at some time during the proceedings. A century after the trials, Janet Batson Davidson, a relative of Batson's, told John Garst, who was researching the Batson ballad (see Appendix D), she had an article from the *Trenton (MO) Times*, dated October 30, 1902, reporting that Ed Batson had attempted a jail break.[1] We were not able to find the article, and Davidson told us she has not been able to locate her copy. But other sources give credence to the possibility of an escape plot.

In November 1902 the *Abbeville Meridional* reported that "Edward Batson, who is incarcerated in the jail at Lake Charles . . . had planned to make his escape by sawing through the iron bars of his cell with a saw made from a number of needles forced through a piece of wood. When discovered, one bar was cut into about an eighth of an inch. There were other prisoners implicated in the attempt. . . . The discovery was made by Jailer Lyons."[2]

The *Welsh Rice Belt Journal* was more specific: "An attempt to escape from the parish jail at Lake Charles was discovered last week . . . [and] it is believed that Batson was the leader of the attempt."[3]

The "unique" plan "had been in operation for several days" before its discovery. "A number of needles were secured and forced through a stick about ten inches long, forming an almost perfect saw." Eight prisoners planned to "saw through the bars of the cage to liberty," but Lyons "had a feeling all week that matters were not as they should be," according to the report.[4]

Lyons "ordered one of the prisoners . . . into the office, and there questioned him thoroughly, until finally the prisoner admitted that plans for a wholesale escape were on foot." Deputies then searched the jail and found the makeshift saw hidden between a bathtub and a wall.[5]

We find no report of the attempt itself in the Lake Charles newspapers, but on November 8, 1902, the *Lafayette Advertiser* reprinted editorial comments from the *Lake Charles Daily American* apparently in retort to an editorial in the Baton Rouge paper.[6]

In the *Advertiser* reprint, the *Daily American* editorial criticized the *Baton Rouge Advocate*, which "seems to have constituted itself the defender of Albert Edwin Batson." The editorial comments in the Lake Charles newspaper were in response to the following in the Baton Rouge paper: "We think it only fair and just that the full facts be well established before an accusation should be made of an attempt to break jail, by a man under indictment for murder. Surely the facts are obtainable. . . . If [Batson] made the attempt to cut his way out of jail, he is entitled to the odium of such a charge, but it seems cruel injustice to add to his other woes by laying this charge at his door, unless investigation has established its verity."[7]

The Lake Charles paper responded sarcastically to the *Advocate's* "solicitude . . . for the amiable Batson's reputation and good name," then continued, "if the officers say that an attempt was made to break jail, and that Batson was probably concerned in it, the Advocate may be content to accept the fact as true, but it really matters [little] either way. Compared to the crime with which he is charged, anything else must appear venial and trivial."[8]

A Missouri newspaper carried the news on August 13, 1903, that Sheriff Perkins arrested three boys who were caught "acting suspiciously." According to that report, "someone saw the lads . . . tie something to a string which hung from the upper window opposite the cell of Batson."[9]

When deputies searched Batson's cell, according to this story, they found a ball of twine with a fork tied to the end of it. Apparently the fork was used as a weight to cause the twine to drop to the ground so that something could be tied onto it. The account identified the three boys as Ben Bonner, John Bonner, and Frank Dailey.[10]

On August 14, 1903, the *Lake Charles Weekly American* reported,

> Ben and John Bonner and Frank Dailey, the three young men accused of trying to pass tools to A. E. Batson, the condemned murderer, charged with attempt to aid an escape from jail, created something of a scene in court this morning when arraigned upon a bill of information by the district attorney charging them with the offense. One of them said, "We plead not guilty," another said, "We never did it," while the third mumbled something about the district attorney being a "d——d liar." . . . Judge Miller was amazed at the impudence of the three youths and intimated [that] when the present charge was disposed of the court would have something to say to them.[11]

A search of newspapers around the dates of the alleged breakout and the trial of the three men brings no other details. Nonetheless, the press noted that "as the time for the execution approaches, the watch kept upon Batson becomes more intense. Few of the many people who apply for admission to the jail succeed in gaining the coveted permission, and even those who do will be searched . . . before being admitted. Sheriff Perkins is devoting his time to Batson, and most of his time is spent in the jail."[12]

That limited access to Batson's cell disappeared during his last days of incarceration. Particularly on the day before his execution, he became, more than he had already been, something akin to a zoo animal—to be looked at, studied, even fed.

On the morning before he was to die, Rev. M. E. Weaver of the First Baptist Church in Lake Charles had "a three minute confidential conversation" with Batson. The sheriff gave "strict orders that while the minister was holding conference with the condemned man no one should be allowed to interfere with them."[13]

Batson told reporters in June he did not belong to any one church, and "if necessary, I can pray for myself as well as anyone else." He added ruefully that while many folks seemed to be praying for him, they had not saved his life. After the minister left, "a small crowd" was let into the jail "to look over the gallows and have a short talk [with] Batson." When he was asked how he felt, he replied, "The same as ever."[14]

In the afternoon, "The largest weekday crowd of inquisitive people entered the prison and took a look at Batson." The *Daily American* reported, "They flocked around the doomed man's cell asking many questions. . . . to which the condemned man replied in a suave manner. He stood erect with his head thrown back, never once trembling or showing any sign of nervousness. He was attired in a nicely fitting pair of trousers, with his shoes shined and hair nicely groomed."[15]

Throughout his last days, people passing his cell would offer him something to eat, which he always refused, pointing out that it was "positively forbidden, as nothing in the way of edibles could be sent him except what was prepared under the supervision of the jailer."[16]

Even in the shadow of the gallows, Batson kept up a ready smile, a hearty appetite, and remained an "enigma to everybody," according to the *New Orleans Picayune*.

> No two persons agreed upon his manner. Some attributed it to bravado, some to callousness, some to a knowledge of his guilt and a sense of the justice of his punishment, while still others held that he was anxious to appear to good advantage. He was a quiet and obedient prisoner, and was satisfied with everything . . . around him, never complaining and always ready and willing to do anything requested of him without a murmur. By his fellow prisoners he was well liked, and all felt sorry for him. He spent considerable time while in prison writing doggerel poetry and songs, and at one time he had serious thought[s] of writing a history of his life. Toward the last he appeared to have been reconciled to [his] fate.[17]

The *Daily American* wrote, "The condemned man faced his audience in an unconcerned manner. . . . Mrs. Payne was present when the large crowd was admitted, sorrowful looking indeed, looking to all as though her heart was broken, and her nerves shattered. Seating herself in an adjoining room . . . she calmly awaited the dispersal of the crowd, when she would be granted the privilege of conversing with her son, face to face, in his cell."[18]

Batson's mother "was thoroughly searched by the sheriff, submitting in a most pleasant manner," the newspaper reported. "What was said [between her and her son] is not known, but the supposition is that she poured out her heart, boiling over with a mother's sympathy."[19]

According to the *Picayune*,

> The poor woman bears up bravely in her misery. After leaving her son Wednesday Mrs. Payne took a stroll around the city for exercise. She is at present stopping . . . more than half a mile from the jail where her son is confined. She refuses absolutely to receive any visitors at her boarding-house, except such ladies as come to offer her sympathy and to condole with her in her misfortune. As to newspapermen, she will not under any circumstances receive any of them, no matter what their opinion in regard to her son may be. The lady with whom she is stopping answers questions and, without consulting Mrs. Payne, refuses to allow any member of the press access to the house. She had doubtless received her instructions from Mrs. Payne and carries them out to the letter.[20]

Batson's lawyers made one last trip to Baton Rouge to seek a reprieve from the governor, arriving on the evening before the execution. They met with Governor Heard for two hours, futilely. After the conference the governor told newsmen, "I have given due and patient consideration to the affidavits, papers, and arguments of Batson's attorneys and have carefully gone over every detail presented and I have been unable to find sufficient justification to reopen this case. I do not consider that what was presented was material sufficient to . . .

change my decision to not interfere with the process of the law and I have notified Batson's attorneys to that effect."[21]

His long-suffering mother brought the bad news to Batson. Before he retired for the night, the *Weekly American* reported, "His mother was admitted [to the jail] with the fateful telegram that bore the news that all hope had departed. He read the telegram silently and handed it back to her without a word or a sign of the deep emotion a man must feel who is face to face with death."[22]

24

To the Gallows

Finally, on the morning of Friday, August 14, 1903, all was in readiness for the hanging of Ed Batson. "The gallows . . . has [*sic*] been erected, and all that is necessary to place it in position for use is to fit it together, the frame being a part of the equipment of the jail," the *New Orleans Picayune* reported. "The drop will be just in front of Batson's cell, and Sheriff Perkins will pull the lever which will release the trap which will drop Batson into eternity."[1] On the day before, "the rope had been stretched and tested, the noose tied, and the mechanism of the trap worked . . . all of which the doomed prisoner watched with unconcern."[2]

Earlier, there had been some speculation that Batson would never see his execution day. The *Lake Charles Daily American* reported in May that "Batson . . . is said to be gradually sinking under the great strain he has been subjected to during the past year and . . . his death would not be a surprise."[3] Apparently there was no basis for that rumor. Batson was in good health and spirits until his final breath.

Deputy Dan Ryan, who slept outside Ed Batson's cell, had a long conversation with him on the night before he was to be hanged. They talked until 3:30 in the morning, Ryan said, and Batson was "sorrowful at times" and at others "just as talkative and happy as if nothing worried him." Batson said it was hard to realize this would be his last night on earth. "I am going to die like a man, walking to the scaffold like the innocent man I am [and] as if I were going to be a spectator of someone else's fate," he told Ryan. He said he believed the two juries that had heard his case were prejudiced and never even considered acquitting him, and he had nothing good to say about the judge.[4]

"There are a great many people around this section who think that Judge Miller is a Christian," Batson told Ryan, "but I want to go on record as saying that he has not a drop of Christianity in his veins."[5]

The condemned man was awakened at 5:45 A.M. by the jailer and said he was feeling fine and that nothing was troubling him. Reverend Weaver visited the cell around 9:00 A.M., staying for about twenty minutes and coming out convinced that Batson would go to his death "as firmly and calmly as ever."[6]

Earlier in the day, Ed Batson had bathed and put on a "neat black suit," and collarless shirt.[7] After putting on his starched white shirt, he hung the collar, which came with it, around the bars of his cell. He put his coat on, and then Deputy Sheriff Richard, who was in the cell with him, thinking that he had forgotten his collar remarked: "Oh, you forgot to put on your collar."

Batson glanced at the place where he had hung the collar up, and said quietly, "No, I didn't. It is not necessary to put the collar on. It will interfere with the rope."[8]

According to the *New Orleans Picayune*, Batson's mother arrived for her final visit at ten o'clock, "looking to all as though her heart was broken and her nerves shattered."

> Mrs. Payne . . . accompanied by four lady friends, was at the courthouse early seeking admission, and about 9 o'clock proceeded to the door of the prison. Deputy Sheriff Lyons was on duty and when Mrs. Payne asked to see her son, she was told that the Sheriff had left strict orders not to admit anyone into the prison without his orders. Mrs. Payne and her friends remained outside the prison walls for more than an hour, when finally Sheriff Perkins appeared and the party was then admitted. . . . They ascended to the second floor, where Batson's cell was just at the head of the flight of stairs and facing the gallows. Sheriff Perkins ordered the door of Batson's cell to be opened and the prisoner stepped out and seated himself on the window

> sill, his mother seated opposite him. Their last meeting was most affectionate. Mrs. Payne wept bitter tears, but of audible expressions of grief she did not give vent. Batson hugged and held his mother and his eyes were wet with tears, but he bore up bravely through the ordeal, the most trying, to all appearances, which he underwent.[9]

One of the witnesses to the execution told the reporter from the New Orleans paper that Mrs. Payne asked her son for the last time if he was guilty. "No, I am innocent," he said.[10] Rachel Payne left the jail "crying and sobbing, and with some ladies who had accompanied her, quietly took her departure."[11]

Another of the morning visitors to Ed Batson's cell was Dr. W. L. Fisher, described as "a good friend to Batson," who had been selected as a witness to the execution. According to the *Picayune*, "Dr. Fisher said to Batson that he had a curiosity to know how a man felt in such a condition as Batson now found himself, but that he hesitated to ask him and hoped that he would not take the question amiss." Batson, smiling, told him, "Words could not express to you how I feel. It is a terrible thing. That's about all I can say."[12]

Four newspaper representatives also visited the prisoner on his final morning. They questioned him for fifteen minutes, and "never once did he show any signs of weakening, but always had a little smile playing on his lips."[13]

Batson again brought up one of the questions never answered during his ordeal, asking if any of the missing Earll stock other than the animals found in Lake Charles had ever been recovered. When he was told that none of the other stock had turned up, Batson said, "That shows conclusively that they are hanging the wrong man. For if they had found the other stock, they would have found the man that had committed the murder."[14]

He also denied emphatically that his attorneys had told him to keep silent during any part of the legal battle or now at the end of his life. "They have never told me not to make any statement," he said. "On the contrary, they said if I had anything to say, to say it when I was on the gallows. Not having anything to say in the way of a statement, and I know nothing to tell, you need not expect any statement from me."[15]

According to the *Weekly American*,

> From 11 o'clock until twenty minutes of twelve there was a steady pouring in of inquisitive people wishing to take a last look at the doomed man. Ladies, children, and men trampled on each other in their frantic effort to take a glimpse of the murderer within two hours of death. Owing to the surging crowd enlarging every five minutes, the sheriff brought Batson, at his request, downstairs, in the front northeast corner room of the jail, so that every one could look at him. People hung on the gate, the fence, up signs against trees and every place imaginable to get in a position to see him.[16]

After a few minutes, the sheriff told his prisoner, "Well, Ed, we had better go." Batson told the crowd, "Good-by, boys." He was then given a final meal of some eggs and a little white wine, which he ate "very heartily." The sheriff asked if Batson had any preference for the hour of his execution, which could be carried out at any time between noon and two o'clock.[17] Batson told Perkins he didn't want to dictate the time but, "naturally, I would like all the time coming to me."[18]

From noon until 12:30 P.M., the prisoner was left alone, using some of the time to write letters to his sister and brother, advising his brother, Noah, to never drink, swear, nor gamble. He told his siblings he was innocent of the murders.[19]

"There was no one to disturb his thoughts, excepting occasionally a guard would pass through the small hall facing his cage on some errand, saying not a word, only glancing to make sure the condemned man was still in the cell, which has harbored him for near on to twenty months," the *New Orleans Picayune* reported.[20]

As one of his final wishes, Batson asked that poetry he'd written during his confinement would not be published and that it would be kept out of the newspapers; his request apparently was granted.[21] We have searched for his poems with no success.

By one o'clock on the afternoon of Friday, August 14, 1903, a thousand people or more were gathered outside the Lake Charles jail, even though most of them had no chance of actually witnessing Ed Batson's final moments.

The *Picayune* recorded,

> The scaffold was visible from one side of the prison through a window, while from the other side a view of the doors of Batson's cell could be seen. The largest crowd, of course, assembled on the side nearest the gallows, but they were doomed to disappointment, for a curtain was placed across the window, shutting off the view, and the crowd surged around to the other side. The sun was intensely hot, there was scarcely a breath of air stirring, and the few trees which had been planted in the Courthouse square and along the sidewalks were so crowded with people that the heat was even more intense in the shade of the trees than it was in the sun.[22]

The crowd "stared and blinked at the walls of the prison, which threw off a foggy vapor of steam. . . . Umbrellas were of little use, for when a sunshade was raised men thrust their heads under it, and the owner was made as uncomfortable as could be by the proximity of others. . . . Nothing could be seen, and no one even expected to be able to see anything of what was taking place inside."[23]

Inside the jailhouse were the official witnesses for the execution, including Sheriff Perkins, Dr. T. H. Watkins, Dr. W. L. Fisher, Dr. C. E. Terry, Rev. M. E. Weaver, and chief deputy C. M. Richard.[24]

At 1:20 P.M. Reverend Weaver had a private, three-minute final talk with the condemned man. Then, as the time for the execution drew near, witnesses talked among themselves and with the prisoner. "There is only one time to die and it comes to everybody," Batson said. He said going to be hanged "is much easier than to go to have a tooth pulled . . . having a tooth pulled hurts more and longer."[25]

At 1:30, the sheriff looked at his watch and asked, "Well, Ed are you ready to die?"

Batson replied, "Yes, at any time that it suits you."[26]

The bell in the courthouse tower was tolling the half hour as deputy sheriffs Richard and Foster entered Batson's cell. Richard carried a small piece of new clothesline. Batson placed his hands behind his back, ready for them to be tied, when, in the language of a newspaper report, "he bethought himself and exclaimed. 'Before you tie my hands, I should like to shake hands with you.'"[27]

Richard shook hands with him. Batson then extended his hand to Foster, who also shook hands with him, then he asked to shake hands with Sheriff Perkins and Deputy Lyons. They entered the cell and shook hands with him, and then he shook hands with everyone present. The rope was then tied around his wrists and, "leading the way, Deputy Richard emerged from the cell, followed by Batson with head erect and a fearless expression in his eyes."[28]

At 1:38 P.M. Reverend Weaver stepped onto the platform and offered a short prayer. The sheriff then asked Batson, "Well, Ed, do you want to say anything?" Batson, "cool and composed, more so than the witnesses and deputies," said he had no statement to make. He "stood straight and motionless" as the rope was adjusted around his neck at 1:41 P.M.[29]

Sheriff Perkins, who was the one adjusting the rope, placed the knot under Batson's right ear. According to the press account, "Discovering his mistake as he stepped back, the Sheriff remarked: 'Is it all right?' Batson replied: 'I believe it's all safe.' The Sheriff . . . differed with him, and said: 'No, the knot is on the wrong side. I ought to have put it on the left side.'"[30]

Proper placement of the knot was important, because done correctly, it would break the prisoner's neck; if done incorrectly, he would dangle at the end of the rope, dying slowly by strangulation.

According to the press account, "The error seemed to rather amuse Batson, who smiled faintly . . . [as] the Sheriff, assisted by Batson, moved the knot around to the left side of his neck, when Batson stopped him as he was walking away and asked Perkins to move the knot a little further back so that it should come under his ear."[31]

"Are you ready?" the sheriff asked.

When Batson did not answer, the sheriff stepped to the lever and said, "Well, good-by Ed."[32]

According to the *Picayune*, "Perkins pulled the lever, and simultaneously with the click, Batson . . . exclaimed audibly, 'Good-by,' and the next instant he had dropped."

The trap fell at 1:42 P.M.[33]

The drop was about eight and one-half feet, leaving him suspended eighteen inches from the jail floor. "The body dropped through the trap and swayed violently. A few moments it gyrated, a few last gasps were heard and then the soul of Albert Edwin Batson went to render an account to his Maker."[34]

He was pronounced dead at 1:57 P.M. The sheriff's adjustments to the rope notwithstanding, Batson died of strangulation; the fall did not break his neck. Ed Batson's body was removed from the scaffold at 2:05 P.M. At 3 P.M., witnesses to the execution filed into the courthouse to sign the death certificate.[35]

Ed Batson's body was taken to Swift-Kirkwood undertakers, where it was embalmed and prepared for shipment to Spickard, Missouri, by mortician Louis Runte. Part of the expense for his final train ride was borne by the parish and part of it by "sympathetic residents."[36]

The *Daily American* reported, "The remains presented a perfectly natural appearance this morning: the features were composed and tranquil although they had taken on that wax-like appearance peculiar to death and a slight abrasion about the neck was the only sign of the fate he met."[37] The remains were placed in what a reporter described as a "neat" casket and taken to the Kansas City Southern train depot, where his mother was waiting. She had not witnessed the execution.[38]

> The unfortunate lady was pale and careworn and the indelible traces of great grief were stamped upon her features. When the undertaker had seen the casket stowed away, he shook hands good-by with the stricken woman. Her heart was too full for words but she clung convulsively to his hand, as a child might,

> until the trainmen's call warned her that it was time to get aboard.
>
> And so the scene ends. As the train pulled out the morning sun shone over the city where the Batson tragedy was already being forgotten. All that remained of it was six graves in the Welsh cemetery, and a heart-broken mother journeying home with her dead.[39]

Albert Edwin Batson, who died at the age of twenty-two years, four months, and six days, is buried in Bethel Cemetery, about five miles east of Spickard in Grundy County, Missouri. His mother selected the words that are engraved on his tombstone: "Truth is might and will prevail. God reigns. He is love."[40]

To the end, Ed Batson denied his guilt. As crowds of curious people filed by his cell in the final hours before his hanging, "the question [of his guilt was asked] in various forms," the *Picayune* observed. "He always protested his innocence . . . and his only comment was that he was going to a juster Judge than he had on earth."[41]

On a final note, one of Rachel's granddaughters married a grandson of Joseph Payne, uniting the two families a second time. The young couple moved to Seattle, Washington. Rachel was visiting them when she suffered an abscessed tooth. A dentist extracted it, but it had become infected. She died within a few days of septicemia at barely fifty years old. She now lies in Bethel Cemetery in an unmarked grave next to her son's, the place she chose in a final proclamation of her belief in his innocence.[42]

Afterword

Beyond Reasonable Doubt?

In the United States our system of laws holds that a person accused of wrongdoing is presumed innocent until proven guilty. Many think that principle is part of the U.S. Constitution, but in fact, it predates the Constitution, coming to American jurisprudence from English Common Law.[1] It probably dates from Roman law, embodied in the phrase *Ei incumbit probation qui dicit, non qui negat*, which translates roughly as, the burden of proof rests on the one who asserts, not the one who denies.[2]

Not only must a defendant be proven guilty, it must be beyond reasonable doubt; that is, a juror must have a real reason to find a defendant guilty or innocent of a crime. To meet the legal criterion, any doubt of guilt must be based upon reason and common sense after careful consideration of all the evidence, or lack of evidence, in a case.[3]

Proof beyond a reasonable doubt does not mean absolute certainty, but it does mean the presence of enough certainty that a reasonable person would be willing to accept it and act upon it. A majority of the people of southwest Louisiana believed that the case against Batson met that criterion; some others thought his guilt had not been fully proven, or at least not fully enough to warrant the death penalty.

On the day of his death, the *New Orleans Picayune* reported,

> The story of the murder, the events which led to the accusation against Batson, his flight and arrest in Spickard, Mo., the day after the murder was unearthed . . . his manner, actions and professions of innocence, his lack of a defense, his trial and

> conviction, his appeal for a new trial and the granting of the same by the Supreme Court, and his second trial and conviction reads like a romance. But few people residing in Lake Charles had any doubt of his guilt. . . . A number of people however, doubted that Batson was the guilty party. Some did not think that the guilt had been proven beyond a doubt, and hinged their belief upon his protestations of innocence and the language of the man, and the coolness that he displayed at all times during his two trials, in prison and while conversing with others. Careful guard was set upon him, he was watched day and night, yet not once did he betray either by word or deed any knowledge of the crime.
>
> But there was yet another reason urged by those who would not believe Batson guilty of the crime, and that was the absence of any motive for such a horrible deed. . . . [The stealing of the stock] could not have been his motive. First, there was much more stock on the rice farms than was found in Batson's possession . . . [which] did not form a third of the stock on the place, and [there] was a question of what became of the rest of the stock. . . . It had never been claimed by the State that Batson was searching for money, as it was known to him that Ward Earll invariably deposited his money in the bank in Welsh.[4]

In his charge to the jury, Judge Miller explained that a reasonable doubt is when a specific reason can be found, and that if jurors had such a doubt, it was their duty to acquit Ed Batson. Defense attorneys emphasized that circumstantial evidence is competent evidence under the law, but every circumstance must fit the picture, and, further, it must be found that there are no reasonable circumstances under which someone else could have committed the crime.

Putting ourselves in the place of a juror at that time and place before the introduction of modern crime-solving methods such as DNA testing, would we have found there was sufficient evidence for Albert Edwin Batson to have been hanged? Or would we have had a reasonable doubt?

There is no way to know a century later whether this young stranger from Missouri was guilty or innocent of the Earll murders. We believe, however, that even from this distance of years, a reasonable person can certainly think Ed Batson should not have been hanged, and his sentence should have been no more than life in prison, as the pardon board recommended.

Indeed, it is interesting to speculate whether that might have been the outcome at trial had a decision such as in the case of *Witherspoon v. Illinois* in 1968 been made before 1903. In that case the U.S. Supreme Court held that the death penalty can be invalid if people who object to the death penalty are systematically excluded from the jury.[5] The high court ruled, "In its quest for a jury capable of imposing the death penalty, the State produced a jury uncommonly willing to condemn a man to die."[6]

As in the Batson case, the jury in *Witherspoon* had the option of deciding guilt with or without capital punishment—and, if reports are true, two Batson jurors preferred to recommend life in prison over death. Would a modern jury agree with them? The court said in *Witherspoon* that questions of guilt and questions of punishment are separate, and it is possible that a jury can show no bias in deciding guilt but hold substantial bias in deciding the proper sentence.[7]

In the *Witherspoon* decision, the majority held:

> In this case the jury was entrusted with two distinct responsibilities: first, to determine whether the petitioner was innocent or guilty; and second, if guilty, to determine whether his sentence should be imprisonment or death. It has not been shown that this jury was biased with respect to the petitioner's guilt. But it is self-evident that, in its role as arbiter of the punishment to be imposed, this jury fell woefully short of that impartiality to which the petitioner was entitled. . . . Whatever else might be said of capital punishment, it is at least clear that its imposition by a hanging jury cannot be squared with the Constitution.[8]

The juries in both Batson trials were carefully selected on the basis of their belief in capital punishment based on circumstantial evidence. They probably did not meet *Witherspoon* standards. But even under the rules in play at the time of Batson's trials, significant issues arise.

First, questions remain about when the crime was committed and how that fits with claims by Batson and by his accusers of where he was at the time of the murders. The coroner, Dr. Watkins, testified that decomposition of the bodies made it impossible to say exactly when the Earlls were murdered, and that from the physical evidence he could only estimate the time of death within a five- to twelve-day period. The time of the murder was set as February 13 because Ward Earll had been seen in Welsh on February 12, and because the man with the scar and the mules was seen in the Louisiana town of Iowa on the evening of February 13. But there is no substantial link between either event and the murders, and Ed Batson maintained he was already riding the rails toward Texas on February 13.

Second, when were the different victims killed? It was apparently assumed in all the written material about the murder of the Earll family, and during the Batson trials, that the mother and children were killed before L .S. Earll, based simply on the fact that their bodies were found first.

But if the motive for the murders was money, it is much more likely that L. S. Earll had more of it than his son Ward. The father had the bigger farm, had sold the bigger rice crop, and was probably more conservative with his money than Ward, who was described by some people who knew him as a gambler, drinker, and wastrel. If that was the case, a would-be robber would go to the father first, and he would have been the first one killed. Consider the following scenario as a possibility:

Ward is ill after having stayed too long at the Mardi Gras festivities, and his mother goes to his house to take care of him. The younger boys are at school, which leaves L. S. Earll alone at home. Either by chance or design, someone finds the older man alone and tries to rob him. Earll resists and is shot, then his house is searched for money. Note that L. S. Earll's body was found partially buried, meaning that the killer had taken time to try to dispose of it, which was not the case with the rest of his family.

Upset because he finds nothing, the killer decides to go to Ward's place, where he finds Ward, his mother, and his brother Fay, who had driven Mrs. Earll to Ward's. He kills them and searches the house. Coming home from school, the younger boys stop at Ward's while the search is going on, surprise the killer/robber, and are themselves murdered. Finding no money at Ward's either, the killer/robber takes what stock he can find to try to sell it for what he can get.

This scenario does not necessarily clear Batson, primarily because if he was on the farm that day, he would have known the older Earll was alone, giving Batson the opportunity to rob him. It also assumes that the killer knew that Ward Earll lived separately from the rest of the family. But it does provide a plausible alternative version of the crime that could be used to raise a reasonable doubt about the prosecution's theory of what happened.

Questions also remain about Batson's facial scar and the scarred man seen with mules and horses in the neighboring town of Iowa on February 13. Charles Dobson in his book *Guilty? Side Lights on the Batson Case* claims the man with the mules was scarred on the left side of his face, and John Downs said at first that the man who came to his stable was scarred on the left side. However, Batson's scar was on the right side. Witnesses also said the man in Iowa wore a rubber coat (presumably rain apparel), which if it was found was never introduced into evidence. Witnesses at the Lake Charles stable said the man who came in wore overalls and boots; none of them saw a rubber coat, and it was not among those things found in the buggy.

Another question arises over the murder weapon. According to all the testimony, at least four of the Earlls were hit by blasts from a shotgun—but what shotgun? Trial witnesses testified that the man with the scar took a shotgun to a gunsmith after leaving the Downs stable, but a shotgun was found in the buggy that was left at the stable. Deputy Isaac Fontenot testified he found yet another shotgun at the residence of L. S. Earll after the murder, and Maude Earll testified that her father and each of her brothers kept shotguns for hunting. The prosecution never placed any of these shotguns in the hands of Ed Batson, and, having lost samples of the shot, never actually connected any of the guns to the murder itself.

In addition, the prosecution never introduced a knife or any other instrument that could have been used to cut the throats of the victims, nor did it produce evidence that the cut wounds—which bled very little—were actually made at the time the Earlls were killed.

We also wonder why Ed Batson would have stayed around Calcasieu Parish after such a horrible crime. As Dobson notes, "The committing by any man of such a bloody tragedy would naturally induce him to put as great a distance as possible between him and his victims."[9]

Yet, we have testimony that a man believed to be Batson was seen plowing the Earlls' field on the morning of February 13, and horse traders in Lake Charles spoke of a man willing to spend a full day in town dickering over a few dollars for the sale of stock rather than accepting the first good offer and using the money to distance himself from the bloody crime scene. After trying to sell the stock the man alleged to be Batson was seen standing on a street corner, leisurely eating candy or nuts. Does that seem like something a man who should be on the run would do?

Further, prosecutors claimed that the note tacked to Ward Earll's door saying Ward had gone to Lake Charles had been put up by the killer to give him time to flee. But in the scenario presented by the prosecution, if Batson was fleeing, he was taking his time doing it. It would be illogical for him to put up a sign to give himself time to flee and then remain in the vicinity.

Also, during the first days of the investigation, lawmen said two men had seen the note on the door on February 8, five days before the date set by the coroner as the day the Earlls died.[10] That does not square with the theory that Batson put the note on the door on the day of the murders, February 13.

What about the tramp reported to be an accomplice? Did he even exist? Could he have done it? Or perhaps the insane man who was jailed in Clinton was the murderer. Authorities said he confessed to the crime. The fact that he was insane tends to make the possibility of his committing such a brutal murder as that of the Earlls more plausible, not less so.

Where was Fred Earll during all this time? He said he was in Eagle Grove, Iowa, but there is no record of his being there then. He inherited at least part of the farms of his brother and parents, and he claimed to know exactly how much money was taken at the time of the murders, even though he said he was hundreds of miles away.

Again, how did the murderer get out of the room with the bodies of the victims blocking the door, and the windows covered with oilcloth or shuttered and left undisturbed?

Most important, there is the question about the sheer violence of the crime. When everything is boiled down to its essence, Ed Batson was accused of, tried for, and put to death for viciously killing six people for two nondescript horses and four mules, one of which was lame. As noted by the *New Orleans Picayune*, and as the *Crowley Signal* pointed out in its first report of the crime, it is preposterous to think that a man would kill an entire family just to steal some horses and mules that he could have easily stolen without bloodshed.[11]

"Are we to believe," Dobson asks, "that a youth of good reputation and exemplary habits suddenly turns robber and desiring to make his crime atrocious resolved to redden it by carnage? . . . There will always be an argument. There will always be someone who doubts the accuracy of the verdict. There will always be an uncomfortable feeling after this man is executed that perchance he was innocent."[12]

There is little indication in the available record that authorities ever looked for any other possible suspect besides Ed Batson. They seized upon him as the murderer after the very first hearing by the coroner's jury and began to build a chain of evidence based upon their belief in his guilt.

Batson's voice and that of his mother were the only ones heard protesting that someone else committed the horrendous crime. Her protest was made moot, and his voice was made silent on the day of his hanging, because, as Judge Miller had prescribed, Albert Edwin Batson was dead, dead, dead.

1902.

Appendix A: Chronology

1902

February 11

Ward Earll left his house to spend Mardi Gras night in Welsh, leaving Ed Batson in the house two miles from town.

February 12

11 A.M.: Ward Earll was seen alive on the road home.

3 P.M.: John and Lemuel Earll left school in Welsh to go home.

February 13

Neighbor John LeBlanc saw a man he claimed to be Batson driving west two miles from the Earll farm with what was said to be Earll stock. A man with a scar on his face is said to have spent the night in the Louisiana town of Iowa.

February 14

Morning: A man tried to sell four mules and two horses at the Ryan stable in Lake Charles but could not make a deal.

3 P.M.: A man who identified himself as Ward Earll tried to sell the stock to John Downs. Downs and the man met Wells Fargo driver Orrin Mason and gave him a package for delivery to Ed Batson's mother in Spickard, Missouri. In Lake Charles, a man who gave his name as A. E. Batson left a gun to be repaired and a man who gave his name as C. R. Batson had a watch fixed.

February 22

Ed Batson arrived in Spickard.

February 24

4 P.M.: Stock dealer John Downs called Paul W. Daniels of Welsh, telling him he had some mules that were left in Lake Charles by a man purporting to be Ward Earll. Daniels telephoned Maude Earll.

Evening: Maude Earll and a livery driver discovered the bodies of her brothers and mother in Ward Earll's house.

February 25

The body of L. S. Earll was found in a ditch near his home a mile from Ward Earll's cabin.

Ed Batson and his brother, Noah, were arrested in Princeton, Missouri. Noah was quickly released.

February 27

Calcasieu sheriff John A. Perkins left Lake Charles to go to Missouri to bring Batson back to Louisiana.

The box sent to Batson's mother from Lake Charles was opened. It contained nothing but rice.

February 28

Sheriff Perkins arrived in Spickard, Missouri.

March 3

Sheriff Perkins left Missouri with Ed Batson.

March 5

Sheriff Perkins reached New Orleans where he put Batson in jail.

March 10

Judge E. D. Miller called a special session of the Calcasieu Parish grand jury to consider the Batson case.

March 15

John Downs picked out Batson from a crowd at the New Orleans jail and said he was the man who left the Earll stock at his barn.

March 18

Batson is brought from New Orleans to Lafayette, en route to his arraignment in Lake Charles.

March 19

Ed Batson was brought to Lake Charles and appeared at his arraignment. Three Calcasieu Parish men failed to identify him in a jail yard lineup.

March 20

Trial was formally set for April 14.

April 12

Ed Batson's mother arrived in Lake Charles, staying at a local boarding hotel.

April 14

The first trial began with jury selection.

April 16

Testimony began in the first trial.

April 21

The jury returned a guilty verdict.

Maude Earll married Charles K. Ingram of Orange, Texas.

April 30

Judge Miller overruled a motion for a new trial and sentenced Ed Batson to death.

June 10

Defense attorneys argued Batson's appeal before the Louisiana Supreme Court.

June 21

The supreme court reversed the trial court verdict and ordered a new trial.

November 11

Defense attorneys moved for a change of venue, seeking to move the trial away from Lake Charles.

December 11

The Calcasieu court heard arguments on a change of venue.

December 12

Judge Miller denied the change of venue motion.

1903

March 6

The second trial began.

March 12

The jury deliberated only two hours before returning another guilty verdict.

March 13

Defense attorneys announced that they would not appeal the second trial verdict.

March 19

Ed Batson was again sentenced to death.

June 12

Gov. William Heard set Friday, August 14, as the execution date.

July 27

The state pardon board recommended a commutation of sentence, because, according to two of its members, there was not enough evidence to warrant the death penalty.

August 10

Batson's mother met with Governor Heard. He refused to sign a commutation order.

August 13

Governor Heard turned a deaf ear to a final appeal from Batson's lawyers. Judge Miller does the same to a plea for clemency from Batson's mother.

August 14

1:43 P.M.: Ed Batson was hanged.

1:57 P.M.: Ed Batson was pronounced dead.

August 15

Batson's mother boarded a train with the remains of her son to take him back to Missouri for burial.

c. 1910

Rachel Payne, about fifty years old, died in Seattle, Washington, while visiting relatives.

Appendix B: Cast of Characters

Abney, John

A juror in the second trial.

Andrus, Jesse

A juror in the first trial, from the town of Jennings.

Azbel, William

A deputy who assisted Mercer County sheriff John Cook with the Batson arrest in Missouri.

Bailey, George A.

Editor of the *Vinton Herald* who testified that he had been in Welsh at the time of the killings and that the gloves that had been introduced as evidence against Batson were actually used by one of the men moving the bodies from Ward Earll's house.

Batson, Albert Edwin

The accused.

Batson, Charles Ransome

A first cousin of the accused, to whom Ed Batson's only surviving letters were addressed. Charles was the son of Susan Ann Stottlemyre, sister of Batson's mother.

Batson, Cora Mae

See Vredenburg, Cora Mae.

Batson, James Noah

Brother of the accused who was arrested with him in Missouri but quickly released. He died in 1963.

Batson, John W.

Father of the accused. He died in 1950 in Missouri.

Bell, A. E.

Owner of the store in Welsh where Maude Earll worked. During the trials, he testified about a note allegedly attached to the door of Ward Earll's home.

Beyer, Daniel

Juror in the first trial, from Westlake.

Blackford, Samuel

Witness in both trials; a neighbor who testified about when he had last seen the Earlls alive and described the scene when he saw them dead. He had formerly lived in Ward Earll's house and described the premises.

Bonner, Ben and John

Two of the three young men accused of trying to pass tools to Ed Batson in his jail cell.

Breaux, Joseph Arsenne

The Louisiana Supreme Court justice who dissented in overturning Batson's first trial. He was born in Iberville Parish, practiced law in Lafayette and New Iberia, and before his appointment to the state's high court was elected state superintendent of public instruction, the equivalent of today's superintendent of education.

Breaux, Theodule

Juror in the second trial.

Breck, Henry

An Earll neighbor who testified at both trials about finding the piece of paper that had apparently been tacked to Ward Earll's door. He is identified as Henry Precht in reports of the second trial.

Bryan, J. E.

A witness to the execution.

Capps, J. M.

Juror in the second trial.

Caruthers, J. S.

A witness to the execution.

Clark, Ed M.

A rice farmer from Welsh and a witness at Ed Batson's first trial who testified he recognized two of the mules at John Downs's stable as belonging to Ward Earll.

Cogney, William

A Lake Charles man who claimed Batson had tried to sell him Earll stock well before February.

Cook, John T.

Sheriff of Mercer County, Missouri, who arrested Ed Batson in Princeton, Missouri.

Coon, F. W.

A character witness at Ed Batson's second trial. He was a probate judge in Princeton, Missouri, who testified that Ed Batson was known for "peace and quietness."[1] After the second trial he said Batson got a fair hearing.

Courtney, Joe

A witness to the execution.

Dailey, Frank

One of three young men accused of trying to pass tools to Ed Batson in his jail cell.

Dale, Jack

One of the men Batson claims to have met in Welsh before boarding a freight for Beaumont, Texas.

Daniels, Paul W.

Welsh business owner who was called when the Earll mules were brought to Lake Charles under suspicious circumstances.

Delaney, Charles

Juror in the second trial.

Dockery, Alexander Monroe

Governor of Missouri at the time of the murders.

Dobson, Charles

Journalist who wrote a book about the Batson case.

Downs, John

The Lake Charles horse and mule dealer who was suspicious about mules offered to him by someone purporting to be Ward Earll. He signed a petition to have Batson's sentence commuted to life in prison.

Dugan, Belsar

Reportedly the name of a tramp a Washington, DC, newspaper claimed helped Batson kill the Earlls. His name never surfaced at either of Batson's trials. He was also identified as Belisan Dugan by the newspaper in Abbeville, Louisiana.

Earll, Fay

A victim, the third eldest son, eighteen years old. He was born in November 1882.

Earll, Fred

The oldest Earll son, born in April 1874, who was said to be living in Eagle Grove, Iowa, at the time of the murders. He worked for a number of years as a surveyor for the Ogle Map Making Company of Chicago. He died in 1950 in Iowa.

Earll, John

The fourth son, a victim, sixteen years old. He was the last Earll sibling to be born in the state of Iowa in October 1884.

Earll, Lavantia (Mrs. John W.)

Sister-in-law of L. S. Earll, who was present at the first trial. Née Lavantia White, she was the sister of Mary White Earll, who was one of those found dead in Ward's house. She died in 1944 in Boone, Iowa.

Earll, Lemuel (Lemmie)

The youngest son, a victim, about thirteen years old. He was born in March 1889, the only Earll child born in Louisiana.

Earll, Lemuel Sheldon

The Earll patriarch, a victim. He was found dead in a ditch one day after the other Earll bodies were discovered. He was born in July 1847 in New York State and was fifty-five years old when he died in February 1902.

Earll, Mary (Mrs. L. S.)

The Earll matriarch and mother of six, a victim, found clubbed to death in Ward Earll's house. Born Mary White in November 1851 in New York State, she was fifty years old at the time of her death. She married L. S. Earll on August 31, 1871.

Earll, Maude

The only daughter of Mr. and Mrs. L. S. Earll, who discovered the bodies. Although 1900 census records list her occupation as a music teacher, she was a store clerk in Welsh at the time of the murders. She was born in April 1879 and was twenty-three years old in 1902. She married Charles K. Ingram of Orange, Texas, on the day of the first verdict. She died in 1952 in the Los Angeles area, where she and Charles moved in the 1920s.

Earll, Ward

The second Earll son and eldest boy of the victims. He was born in February 1876 and had just turned twenty-six.

Eastman, A. V.

Manager for North America Land & Timber Co., who identified a land contract during the first trial.

Elender, George W.

Juror in the first trial, from Westlake.

Elstner, J. C.

An accountant called as a handwriting expert in the first trial but was not allowed to testify after the defense argued that he was not expert at distinguishing handwriting.

Estopinal, Albert Sr.

Lieutenant governor of Louisiana and one of the two pardon board members who voted to commute Ed Batson's sentence to life in prison. A sugarcane planter from St. Bernard Parish, he served in both houses of the Louisiana legislature between 1876 and 1900 and represented Louisiana's first U.S. congressional district from 1908 until his death at the age of seventy-four.

Farris and Frazier, Mesdames

Two women who gave last-minute affidavits in 1903 claiming they saw someone other than Ed Batson trying to sell the Earll stock.

Findlay, A. J.

Canal superintendent who lived in the town of Iowa and testified in both trials that Batson had come to his house on the night of February 13 and asked to stay overnight in the Findlay barn. He said Batson and another man named

Jim Glover took refuge in the barn for the night. Findlay was a native of the state of Iowa.

Fisher, Dr. W. L.

A local doctor who befriended Batson and was a witness to the execution. He graduated from Tulane University Medical School in 1895 and established a practice in Lake Charles in 1900. He succeeded Dr. T. H. Watkins as Calcasieu Parish coroner and held the position for twenty-eight years. A biography identifies him as "a kindly, generous-hearted man who endeared himself not only to his patients but the general public and all those whose work brought them in contact with him." He was the leading obstetrician in the area for many years. He retired from practice in 1935 and died on March 7, 1937.[2]

Fontenot, Isaac "Ike"

Calcasieu sheriff's deputy who participated in the investigation, testified at both trials, and was a witness to the execution. He bought some of the Earll land when it was later sold at auction. He became the second sheriff of Jefferson Davis Parish after it was separated from Calcasieu.

Fontenot, P. F.

Witness in both trials who testified about when he last saw the Earlls alive.

Foster, D. F.

A witness to the execution.

Foster, James Alton

A juror in the first trial, from Lake Charles.

Fulling, Oscar

A witness at both trials who testified that Batson looked like the man who had tried to sell mules, but he wasn't sure.

Gauthier, L. S.

A saloon owner and witness in both trials who said Batson and Ward Earll had played cards in his saloon in December 1901 and that he saw Batson again on February 14 in front of the First National Bank in Lake Charles with "a bunch of horses and mules."[3]

Gill, H. C.

Calcasieu Parish clerk of court. He is sometimes identified as C. H. Gill.

Glover, James

Man who testified in both trials that he worked for A. J. Findlay and that Batson spent a night in Findlay's barn in the town of Iowa.

Green, E. H. Jr.

Juror in the first trial, from Westlake.

Grimaldi, J. A.

Juror in the first trial, from Westlake.

Groates, William

A witness at Ed Batson's second trial who testified only that the cabin where the bodies were found was Ward Earll's residence.

Guion, Lewis

A state attorney who assisted in the prosecution of the Batson case. His first name is spelled Louis in some reports.

Guion, Walter

Louisiana attorney general who was one of two pardon board members who voted to commute Ed Batson's sentence to life in prison. Born near Thibodaux in Terrebonne Parish, he practiced law in New Orleans until his death there in 1927.

Gunn, R. J.

Lake Charles merchant who testified in both trials that he saw Batson at the Ryan stables about noon on February 14.

Hardy, Thomas S. "Tom"

One of the deputy sheriffs sent to Welsh at the time of the murder.

Harman, Dan

A Calcasieu deputy who accompanied Ed Batson's mother on her first visit to her son in the Lake Charles jail.

Heard, William Wright

Governor of Louisiana from 1900 to 1904 who refused to commute Batson's sentence. He was elected to the Louisiana House of Representatives representing Union Parish in 1884, and to the Louisiana Senate in 1888. In 1892 Heard was elected to the first of two four-year terms as state auditor. Heard was inaugurated governor on May 8, 1900. He died in 1926.

Hebert, Lastie

A witness in both trials who testified that Batson bought some whiskey from his saloon in the town of Iowa on February 13.

Henderson, Johnny

One of the men Batson claims to have met in Welsh before boarding a freight for Beaumont, Texas.

Hewitt, T. N.

A witness to the execution.

Hill, James

Juror in the second trial.

Hoag, H. H.

Juror in the first trial, from Jennings.

Hoffman, J. H.

A witness to the execution.

Ingram, Charles K.

Wallpaper and paint sales representative who married Maude Earll. After moving to the Los Angeles area with Maude in the 1920s he listed himself as an interior decorator.

Johnson, Ben

Employee at Ryan's livery stable who testified at the first trial that he saw Ed Batson at the stable around the middle of February with horses and mules.

Jones, Thomas

A witness in both trials who testified he saw Ed Batson in the Louisiana town of Iowa on the morning of February 14 with two teams of mules and two horses. He was a native of the state of Iowa.

Kelly, N. L.

A witness at both trials who said he had seen a notice on the south door of Ward Earll's house about February 14.

Kimble, J. D.

Blacksmith in Welsh who testified in both trials that he had worked on a shotgun introduced in evidence and that it belonged to John or Fay Earll.

LeBlanc, John

A neighbor who lived about two miles from the Earll farm who testified in both trials that he saw Ed Batson driving down the road on February 13 with the Earll horses and mules.

LeBleu, J. C.

A witness to the execution.

Leveque, D. A.

Juror in the first trial, from Lake Charles.

Lyons, D. C.

A Calcasieu sheriff's deputy who testified at the first trial about finding the vest allegedly belonging to Batson in the buggy left at the stable and at the second trial that a vest intended for introduction as evidence was not the vest that he found. He was a witness to the execution.

Lyons, Horace

One of the deputy sheriffs sent to Welsh at the time of the murder.

Marcantel, David

Juror in the first trial.

Martin, Will

Witness in both trials who testified that he saw Ed Batson at Downs's stable and that he recognized Ward Earll's black horse among the stock that was up for sale.

Mason, Orrin

Wells Fargo driver who testified that a man in the company of John Downs gave him a box on February 14 to be delivered to Mrs. Payne in Spickard, Missouri. Like many of the principals in this case, he was a native of the state of Iowa.

McAffery, William

Owner of Mack's Tavern in Welsh where Batson said he spent time while waiting for a train to take him to Beaumont.

McFatter, J. W.

A witness to the execution.

Meyer, Adolph

One of the Calcasieu Parish men who failed to identify Batson in a lineup.

Meyer, Walter

Another of the men who could not pick Batson out of a lineup.

Miller, Judge E. D.

Presiding judge at both trials and dissenting member of the board of pardons who was adamant that Batson was guilty and should be put to death.

Mitchell, A. R.

A state attorney who assisted the Calcasieu district attorney in prosecuting the case. He was noted for his oratorical skills.

Monroe, Frank A.

Louisiana Supreme Court justice who wrote the opinion overturning Batson's first conviction.

Moore, G. D.

A witness to the execution.

Moore, Joseph

Calcasieu Parish district attorney who prosecuted Ed Batson in both trials. He was in his early thirties at the time of the trials.

Oliver, D. W.

Juror in the first trial, from Westlake.

Overton, Winston

The Lake Charles city attorney who was a Batson defense lawyer. He was a native of Marksville. He later became a state district judge and still later was named to the Louisiana Supreme Court.

Payne, Flavius Josephus

Rachel Stottlemire Batson's third husband.

Payne, John

Batson's stepbrother who met Batson when he returned to Missouri.

Payne, Rachel Stottlemire Batson

Ed Batson's mother.

Perkins, Deputy C. B.

A witness to the execution.

Perkins, John A.

Sheriff of Calcasieu Parish.

Precht, Henry

See Breck, Henry.

Prentice, M.

A witness to the execution.

Price, T. E.

A witness to the execution.

Pugh, W. J.

Juror in the second trial.

Redeke, Nettie

Welsh schoolteacher and a witness at both trials, who testified about when the younger boys were last seen in school. The name is variously spelled Radeke, Radecke, Redeke, and Redicke in news accounts.

Reese, H. L.

Foreman of the Lake Charles streetcar line who testified that he nearly ran into the man selling the mules and that he was not Batson.

Reynolds, Edwin

Juror in the second trial.

Richard, Charles M.

Chief deputy of the Calcasieu Parish Sheriff's Department who investigated the crime, testified in both trials, and witnessed the execution.

Roberts, Frank

Cashier at Calcasieu National Bank called at the first trial as a handwriting expert.

Robertson, Mary (Nettie), Robinson, Marie

She is identified as Mary Robertson in reports of the first trial and Marie Robinson in reports of the second trial. She was a clerk with Maude Earll at Bell's store in Welsh who testified that she sold shotgun shells to Ed Batson sometime in February.

Rock, Herman

Testified in the second trial that he did not recognize Batson as the man he saw trying to sell mules at Ryan's stable. He was a native of the state of Iowa.

Russell, William P. Jr.

One of the men who failed to pick Batson out of a jail yard lineup.

Ryan, Dan

Calcasieu sheriff's deputy who slept outside Batson's cell on the night before the execution.

Ryan, J. Ed

Liveryman from Lake Charles who testified in both trials that Ed Batson brought horses and mules to his stable on February 14.

Sanders, Allen

Juror in the second trial.

Sanford, J. T.

A witness to the execution.

Savoie, D. D.

Juror in the first trial, from Jennings.

Schooler, Mayor Perry

Mayor of Spickard, Missouri, who ordered Batson's arrest after receiving a telegram from Louisiana requesting him to do so.

Shattuck, S. O.

A witness to the execution.

Shultz, H. L.

Juror in the second trial.

Simmons, J. M.

Jury foreman in the second trial.

Sompayrac, Paul

The Batson defense attorney who had the difficult task of finally telling Ed Batson that there was no further hope for commutation and that he would be hanged. He was a native of Natchitoches. After the Batson trial he moved his practice to New Orleans and later became an assistant attorney general for Louisiana. He died in New Orleans of the effects of congestive heart failure on November 24, 1933, at the age of sixty-six.

Stine, Jasper

Juror in the second trial.

Stottlemire, Rachel

Maiden name of Ed Batson's mother, who was Mrs. F. Joseph Payne at the time of the trial.

Strother, S. E. A.

Juror in the second trial.

Sullivan, Paul

Jury foreman in the first trial, from Lake Charles.

Temple, Jim

One of the men Batson claims to have met in Welsh before he boarded a freight for Beaumont, Texas.

Terry, Dr. C. E.

A witness to the execution.

Turner, Flagman (First name unknown)

The train flagman who identified Batson as a man who had taken a through passenger train from Beaumont to Kansas City. He did not testify at either trial.

Vredenburg, Cora Mae Batson

The sister that Ed was visiting in Princeton, Missouri, at the time of his arrest. She was five years older than Ed.

Watkins, Dr. Thomas H.

Calcasieu Parish coroner who held an inquest, testified in both trials, and witnessed the execution. A native of Mississippi, he received his medical degree from Tulane and established a practice in Lake Charles in 1895. He retired in 1949, shortly before his death from cancer at the age of seventy-seven.[4]

Weaver, Rev. M. E. or M. K.

Pastor of the First Baptist Church who counseled Ed Batson at the last. He is identified as M. E. Weaver in one report, M. K. in another.

Welsh, H. K.

A witness to the execution.

West, James

A witness at the second trial who testified about examining the buggy.

Willard, R. P., or K. P.

Witness in both trials, a neighbor from Welsh who testified about when he last saw the Earlls alive. He is identified as R. P. Willard in reports of the first trial and K. P. Willard in reports of the second.

Williams, Dr. (First name unknown)

Acquaintance of Sheriff Perkins who was allegedly near the stable in Lake Charles when Batson brought in the mules and horses, was in New Orleans when the sheriff received news of the murder and was able to tell him where to find Batson, and who accompanied the sheriff when Batson was returned from Missouri. He was identified in newspapers as "formerly a member of the Texas Rangers and a man thoroughly acquainted with detective work."[5] However, he did not testify at either trial.

Williamson, D. C.

A Lake Charles gunsmith who testified in both trials that about the middle of February a man identified as C. R. Batson brought a gun to his shop for repair.

Winterhalter, Otto

A Lake Charles jewelry store owner who testified in both trials that he repaired a watch for W. B. Earle in January 1901 and that the same watch was brought into his shop on February 14, 1902, by a man who gave his name as A. E. Batson.

Appendix C: Batson Letters

Batson family member Catherine Todd has copies of four letters Ed Batson wrote between his two trials. They portray a man concerned with the affairs of his family and who believed that if the trial was moved from Lake Charles to an impartial place he would be found innocent.

* * *

Lake Charles
11.29,02
Mr. C[harles] Batson
Spickards, Mo.
Dear Cousin,

I received your letter some time ago [and] was glad to hear from you and to learn that the folks are all well.

This leaves me as well as ever and feeling real fresh this morning.

The weather has been cool for several days and there is no prospect of its altering soon.

Well Charley, I am glad you have bought your self a farm and hope you will prosper by it, which I believe you will. You people up there may thank God for your crops for there was a great failure down here this year [and] lots of the farmers didn't get half their seed they planted back.

Well Kid, I am going to try and get a change of venue on the 12 of Dec.

I hope you will get some good out of your [race?] mare you have bought. I would like to see her. I'll bet she is a dandy.

Oh, yes, how is our dog getting along? When you write tell me all. You never did say anything about her and I would like to know whether she was any good or not.

You said you had wrote three times. I got two letters from you and some papers and answered both of them and never got any more until the other day.

Well Charley, now will half to excuse this writing for I have two more to write before breakfast and it is nearly that time now.

Tell Myrtle and the children I said hello and that I would like to see them.

All the best. Kiss the children for me and tell Myrtle I read all of those papers she sent me [and] would like to get some more if it wasn't two much trouble.

Well by by for this time. I will close hoping to hear from you soon. I am your troubled cousin.
A. E. Batson

* * *

Lake Charles, La.
Dec. 8, 1902
Mrs. Myrtle Batson
Spickards, Mo.
Dear Cousin,

I received your letter some time last week [and] was so glad to hear from you and to learn that you were all well.

Well your papers haven't come yet but may come any time. I have lots of papers since I have been here and find that the Advocate [newspaper] is all right. I like to get it real well and hope you will continue to send it to me.

Well Myrtle, I am glad that Charley has bought him self a farm for you won't half to [be] bothered moving around any more.

I think Edgar is doing real well in his schooling and I am glad he likes to go, for if he likes to go he will shurley learn fast.

Well it is cloudy down here and looks like it was going to rain. It doesn't do very much else but rain down here. I wish it would take and snow some for a change.[1]

Well I go out for to see if I can get my change of venue. I hope I get it but that I can't tell.

Crops are mostly ruined by too much rain and that is about all you can say about the country. They are doing a right smart of building here in the city and we are going to finish the courthouse by the first of the year.[2]

Well, I will close hoping to hear from you soon.

From your cousin,
A. E. Batson

* * *

Lake Charles, La.
December 8, 1902
Mr. Edgar Batson
Spickards
Little Cousin,

I received your letter [and] was surprised to hear from you but awful glad you did.

I am well and hope this finds you the same.

Well Edgar, you are a learning fast and I hope you will keep it up for I want to see you make a good man. Go to school every time you get the chance and help little Murrell all you can. Be a good boy. Treat all the children well and they will treat you the same.

Kiss the babys for me and remember my advice. Love everybody and you will win.

By-by, from your cousin,
Ed Batson

* * *

Lake Charles, La.
Dec. 8, 1902
Mr. Charles Batson
Spickards, Mo.
Dear Cousin,

I take pencil in hand to let you know that I am well and hope this will find you the same.

Well Charley, it is cloudy here today and looks mighty much like rain. I wish it looked like snow for I look out and see it rain and it makes me think of how it would look if I were up there.

Well Charley, every bit of the rice on some plantations ruined by the rains this fall. How I wish I was up there to hunt chickens and quail. I know we would have a good time with our dog.

I got a letter from home the other day and they were all well. Noah is working in the R.R. round house at Trenton. Cora's family were all well but little Gilbert. He was sick with the croup.

Well Chas., I have not heard from your mother nor from Bessie since I have been in this trouble. I guess they have forgotten me or else don't know where I am. I am glad your father is getting along so fast for he was always so good to me that he seems nearly like a father to me.

Well Chas., I go out to see if I get a change of venue Thursday. Then I will wrote to you again.

I am glad your crops were good this year and glad you have bought a farm for it will save you lots of trouble and lots of moving around.

Well Chas., if nothing happens I will be [there] to see you in early spring and then we will have fun enough for all the past time. I am having a good time with a kid from [illegible] he is a corker. I tell you most of the boys are trying to make friends but he says they can't fool him.

Well kid, it is not a very long letter that I write this time but I guess it will do.

Oh yes, I think Edgar is doing real well with his schooling, don't keep him out of school but let him go and learn and he will be a boy that you will always be proud of.

Well I must close hoping to hear from you soon.

My love to the children.

Your cousin,

A. E. Batson

Appendix D: The Batson Ballad

In the summer of 1934, John and Alan Lomax recorded a handful of songs played and sung by an unnamed string band led by Wilson Jones, one of several singers who sometimes used the name "Stavin' Chain."[1]

According to Joshua Caffery, recipient of the Alan Lomax Fellowship in Folklife Studies at the Library of Congress, "The Lomax recordings are the only known documentation of this somewhat mysterious ensemble. Who exactly these musicians were, where they might have performed, and who might have been their audience remains a mystery."[2]

Details about the life of Wilson Jones are equally elusive. According to Caffery, he could have been a Wilson Jones who was from the south Louisiana town of Opelousas, and who was drafted into the army to fight in World War I at the age of nineteen in September 1918.[3]

The Batson ballad, Caffery says, is in the tradition of Anglophone black string bands that were heavily influenced by blues music. These bands "have not survived in south Louisiana, [but] the Lomaxes' documentation . . . suggests that the folk blues was a part of the state's cultural landscape up until at least the early part of the twentieth century."[4] Caffery describes the ballad as "a sympathetic . . . tale of a wrongfully accused underdog."[5]

The lyrics are not exactly factual. For example, the ballad gives Batson, who was a single man, a wife and child. However, it is evident the lyrics are based on the real event. Also, Stavin' Chain said Batson was a white day laborer, accused of murdering his employer and his whole family. In Jones's version, the victims were found in an open field with only a little red soil thrown over their bodies.[6]

"While Jones's ballad obviously diverges sharply from the facts as presented at trial," Caffery points out, "many of these divergences relate to details . . . no doubt refigured by oral tradition. . . . The metamorphosis of the Batson story [as reflected in the ballad] . . . is in keeping with its assimilation into the narrative blues tradition—a tradition that tends to invert societal norms, often making heroes of reputed scoundrels. The tune and structure of the song . . . are drawn directly from the widely known African-American folksong, 'Frankie and Johnny,' a song that also presents a generous defense of a murderer."[7]

In Caffery's view, the ballad "is a highly unified, extremely realistic narrative drawn from real events."[8]

The Ballad

Batson been working for Mr. Earle Six long years today,
And ever since he been working for Mr. Earle, He never have got a pay.
(REFRAIN): Crying, "Oh, Mamma, I didn't done the crime."

Batson asked Mr. Earle, Can he take a walk,
Mr. Earle answered Batson, "You can go and come right back."
(REFRAIN)

Batson hitched up Mr. Earle's Two bay horse and a wagon,
Took it back uptown to get him a load of feed.
(REFRAIN)

When he got back to the house, unhitched those two bay mares,
And he walked on back uptown, See something he really liked.
(REFRAIN)

He was walking down Ryan Street looking down in the showcase,
He thought he had something, Something what he really need.
(REFRAIN)

'Bout the time he was looking in the showcase here come Mr. Henry Reese,
Mr. Sheriff, police come a-walking, Throwed two forty-fives in his face.
(REFRAIN)

Mr. Henry Reese's deputy come a-runnin', slapped him across the face,
Says, "Stick 'em up, Batson, for we constitute you under arrest."
(REFRAIN)

Batson asked Mr. Henry Reese, "What you arresting me for?"
Says, "That's all right, Batson, You know all about it yourself."
(REFRAIN)

'Rested poor little Batson, they took him to the county jail,
And then the people begin to gather from miles and miles around.
(REFRAIN)

When Batson got in the jailhouse, locked up in the place,
He took a pencil right in his hand, he marked every day he laid.
(REFRAIN)

Batson told Mr. Sheriff, "Don't you know that's wrong?
You got me charged guilty unfriendly, And I know I ain't done the crime."
Cryin', "Oh, Mamma, I never harm no one."
(REFRAIN)

Batson begin to cry, tell you what he did do,
You could hear old Batson crying Just like a baby child.
(REFRAIN)

The day Batson cried, This is the words he said,
"You're trying me for murder, And I know I never harmed no one."
(REFRAIN)

Well, the judge found him guilty, The clerk he wrote him down,
The jurymen passed the sentence, Poor Batson, he had to be hung.
(REFRAIN)

Batson begin to wonder, Batson begin to moan,
Batson told his people, "You just have to leave your home."
(REFRAIN)

"You may bring me coffee, You may bring me tea,
You got to bring me everything I want 'cept that black jailhouse key."
(REFRAIN)

"Now you may dress in red, You may dress in black,
You may dress any color you want, But you'll never bring Batson back."
(REFRAIN)

Batson's little girl begin to wonder, Batson's little girl begin to cry,
Batson's little child begin to ask him, "Daddy, what they going to do with you?"
(REFRAIN)

Batson's mother cried, Batson's sister cry,
Batson's sister asked him, "When you coming back again?"
(REFRAIN)
They brought poor Batson to the gallows, they brought him back to the hall,
Batson asked the judge if they going to take his life.
(REFRAIN)

Batson asked the judge Was they going to take his life
Judge asked Mr. Batson, "Haven't you done that crime?"
(REFRAIN)

Batson begin to moan, Batson begin to groan,
Batson begin to tell those people He'd never see home no more.
(REFRAIN)

Batson told his brother, the day they brought him back at home,
Says, "If your brother has to lose his life, I tell you what I want you to do."
(REFRAIN)

Batson asked the sheriff, he asked him that two, three times,
Says, "All I want you to do for me, take care of my two little girls."
(REFRAIN)

Batson's mother cried, Batson's mother cried,
Batson's mother had tears a-running clean out of her eyes.
(REFRAIN)

They brought him home to the gallows, they brought him back to the jail,
He started looking around over the people, To see 'em for the last, last time.
(REFRAIN)

They brought his coffin. The day he come to die.
And he told the sheriff, "That's the last thing I'm going to lay down."
(REFRAIN)

Then the priest told Batson, "Black box takes you down,"
Says, "Here comes your black box, You'll never rise again."
(REFRAIN)

They put a black bonnet above his head, they put a rope right on his neck,
They put handcuffs on his hands, balls and chains on his foot.
(REFRAIN)

The people begin to cry, "Umm-mm-mm, Um-mmmm-mmmm,
Poor Batson he is dead and gone."
(REFRAIN)

The clear blood run out of his eyes, nobody they couldn't see his face,
Had a tongue stuck out out of his mouth, six inches long.
(REFRAIN)

A rubber-tired buggy, Decorated horse,
You know they brought Batson to the graveyard, Says, they brought his family back.
(REFRAIN)

His wife walked up to the grave, Fell down on her knees,
Says, "Lord, have mercy," Says, "Batson, are you gone?"
(REFRAIN)

Batson's wife began to pray, pray as hard as she could.
Prayed so much until it looked like The Lord done answered her prayer.
(REFRAIN)

I thought I heard somebody say awhile before she left,
Says, "You're goin' leave me, But I'll meet you some lonesome day."
(REFRAIN)

Batson's little girl cry, Batson's little child cry,
That's all he asked them people, "Take keer of them two little girls."
(REFRAIN)

Um-mmm, Um-mmm-mmm, Um-mmm,
The tears run out of his eyes.
(REFRAIN)

Think I heared somebody say, "Bye-bye, Batson, bye-bye,
Bye-bye, Batson, bye-bye"—And I believe he's dead and gone.[9]

Notes

Preface

1. Lomax's papers and his recording of the ballad made in 1938 near Lafayette, Louisiana, are housed in the Library of Congress, as are the papers of folklorist Robert Gordon, who collected three verses of the song in 1924. The song "Batson" was included in a list of early American ballads compiled by the Library of Congress, but the name of its composer and when it was written are not known. The Lomax recording has been issued on Library of Congress Document DOCD-5675. See Appendix D for the song lyrics.

2. "Batson," sung by Stavin' Chain (Wilson Jones), Lafayette, LA, 1934, recorded by John A. and Alan Lomax, in *Our Singing Country: Folk Songs and Ballads* (New York: MacMillan, 1941), 335–41.

3. Jim Bradshaw, "Batson Murder Trial Was Talk of Parish in 1902," *Lafayette Daily Advertiser*, October 28, 1997, B1.

4. Richard H. Underwood, "The Other Batson Case," *Legal Studies Forum* 31, no. 2 (2007): 766. Underwood is the Spears-Gilbert Professor of Law at the University of Kentucky College of Law. He refers to this as the other Batson case because of the better-known 1986 case of *Batson v. Kentucky*. In that case, the burglary conviction of an African American named James Kirkland Batson was overturned by the U.S. Supreme Court. The high court ruled that a prosecutor's use of peremptory challenge—the dismissal of jurors without stating a valid cause for doing so—may not be used to exclude jurors based solely on their race.

5. Supreme Court of Louisiana, State v. Batson, 32 So. 478, 108 La. 479 (1902).

Prologue

1. "Batson Pays the Death Penalty for His Crime," *New Orleans Picayune*, August 15, 1903, 1.

2. "Due at New Orleans Today," *Lake Charles Weekly American*, March 8, 1902, 5.

Chapter 1

1. "Inhuman Crime at Welsh," *Lake Charles Weekly American*, March 1, 1902, 1.

2. Ibid.

3. "Unshaken on the Brink of Death," *Lake Charles Daily American*, August 13, 1903, 1.

4. At some point all the horses and mules did end up at John Downs's stable. At Ed Batson's first trial, Lake Charles resident Jesse Hutchins testified that he took the horses and mules from Downs's stable and turned them over to liveryman Henry Daigle in Welsh. Daigle testified he bought the horses that had belonged to Ward Earll.

5. "Inhuman Crime," 1.

6. Ibid.; "Death Penalty for Ed Batson," *Lake Charles Weekly American*, April 26, 1902, 3.

7. Underwood, "The Other Batson Case," 766.

8. This is the so-called "Ha Ha letter," transcribed as it appears in *State v. Batson*, 32 So. 478 (La. 1902). We presume that P. D. Plantation refers to the Paul Daniels farm near Welsh where Batson worked for a while.

9. Underwood, "The Other Batson Case," 771. Underwood notes: "This letter reads like a suicide note, and one who would kill might be despondent enough to contemplate suicide—but it is dated in the December before the February murder. Was it dated in error? Did it bear the correct date, and was evidence of a troubled soul? In any event, the circumstances of its discovery and the details provided about Batson's family certainly appeared to point to Batson as the author. On the other hand, a defense lawyer and any dedicated conspiracy theorist would surely claim that the discovery of such a letter was too good to be true. Perhaps it had been planted by the murderer(s) or someone else?"

Chapter 2

1. "Inhuman Crime," 1.

2. "Earll Family Murdered," *New Orleans Picayune*, February 25, 1902, 1.

3. Ibid. An undated clipping from the *Welsh Rice Belt Journal* newspaper contains an advertisement for the Bell store, which reads: "Our general line of merchandise will be kept to the usual high standard, and when in need of Clothing, Dry Goods, Notions, Boots and Shoes, Groceries, etc., etc., call in and see us."

4. "Six Buried in One Grave," *Lake Charles Weekly American*, March 1, 1902, 8.

5. "Inhuman Crime," 1.

6. "The Crime of the Century," *Lake Charles Weekly American*, August 21, 1903, 1, 7; Mrs. Genevieve LeBlanc, current owner of the property, interview by authors, July 31, 2001, Welsh.

7. "Crime of the Century," 1.

8. "Six Buried," 8.

9. "Inhuman Crime," 1.

10. Ibid.

11. "Probably Done Late Thursday," *New Orleans Picayune*, February 25, 1902, 1.

12. "Inhuman Crime," 1. Prosecutors offered a different version of the events at the time of Batson's trial.

13. Underwood, "The Other Batson Case," 768.

14. "Inhuman Crime," 1.

15. "Crime of the Century," 1.

16. Underwood, "The Other Batson Case," 768.

17. "Crime of the Century," 1.

18. "Inhuman Crime," 1.

19. "Batson Pays the Death Penalty," 1; "Kept His Lips Sealed," *Lake Charles Weekly American*, August 21, 1903, 3. China ball trees (*Melia azedarach*) were commonly planted near homes on the treeless southwest Louisiana prairies, sometimes as wind breaks and for shade, but more usually as a source of scarce firewood. They are quick growing, and one-third of the limbs of a tree could be cut each year for firewood. The trees would replenish the cut branches before it was time to cut that portion again. See Walter C. Holmes, *Flore Louisiane* (Lafayette, LA: Center for Louisiana Studies, 1990), 97.

20. Underwood, "The Other Batson Case," 768.

Chapter 3

1. Underwood, "The Other Batson Case," 769.

2. "Six Buried," 8.

3. Ibid. Italics added.

4. Ibid. According to the newspaper report, the coroner's jury consisted of L. E. Robinson, H. E. West, Burt Ivens, J. H. Cooper, and E. M. Powers. Such inquests, or investigations, can be convened by a coroner to look into the cause of a death that was sudden, violent, suspicious, or occurred in prison. Jurors can return verdicts such as natural death, accidental death, death by misadventure, suicide, or murder.

5. Ibid.

6. Ibid.

7. "Inhuman Crime," 1.

8. "Horrible & Gruesome Tragedy Near Welsh," *Crowley Signal*, March 1, 1902, 1.

9. "Inhuman Crime," 1. A lawsuit filed over division of the Earll property in 1904 valued it at $7,470, the equivalent of about $750,000 today. ("For Partition and Accounting," *Lake Charles Daily American*, February 22, 1904, 4.)

10. "Six Buried," 8.

11. "Fresh Evidence against Batson," *St. Louis Republic*, March 25, 1902, 9.

12. "Six Buried," 8.

13. Ibid.

14. Ibid. One deputy theorized later that Ward Earll may have been killed on February 12 after he returned from Welsh and the others on February 13, when the boys returned from school. Underwood, "The Other Batson Case," 770.

15. "Fresh Evidence against Batson," 9.

16. "Earll Family Murdered," *New Orleans Picayune*, February 25, 1902, 1.

17. "Inhuman Crime," 1.

18. Ibid.

19. Ibid.; "Batson Fairly Dealt With," *Welsh Rice Belt Journal*, March 13, 1903, 1. Underwood calls these "interesting reports, because other accounts state that Batson was not well known in the community, and that those who knew him found him quiet and amiable. . . . [while] another article quotes Miss Maud as saying she had always been afraid of Batson." ("The Other Batson Case," 770; "Batson's Tissue of Falsehoods," *Lake Charles Weekly American*, March 8, 1902, 2.)

20. "Inhuman Crime," 1.

21. Ibid.

22. Ibid.

23. "Horrible & Gruesome Tragedy," 1.

24. "Six Buried," 8. It should be noted that newspapers at the time took more liberty with name calling and wild accusations than is legally allowable today.

25. Ibid.

Chapter 4

1. "Earl Home the Scene of Previous Murders," *Washington (DC) Times*, April 17, 1902, 1. There was another murder in 1928 involving several family members in the house that was occupied in 1902 by L. S. Earll. Some Welsh residents interviewed for this book confused that murder with the Batson murder.

2. Ibid.

3. Charles Dobson, *Guilty? Side Lights on the Batson Case* (New Orleans: L. Graham, 1903), 9–10.

4. Ibid., 10.

5. Donald Millet Sr., "The Economic Development of Southwest Louisiana, 1865–1900" (doctoral dissertation, Louisiana State University, 1964). Pages not numbered.

6. Henry M. Brackenridge, *Views of Louisiana* (Pittsburgh, PA: Cramer, Spear, and Eichbaum, 1814), 300.

7. Millet, "Economic Development of Southwest Louisiana."

8. Ibid.

9. William Henry Perrin, *Southwest Louisiana Historical and Biographical* (New Orleans: Gulf Publishing, 1891), 145.

10. Homestead Act, Pub. L. No. 37-64, 12 Stat. 392 (1862).

11. Millet, "Economic Development of Southwest Louisiana"; abstract of title in possession of current owner Genevieve LeBlanc.

12. Nola Mae Ross, "Gigantic Vision Drowned in Salty Water," *Lake Charles American Press*, April 20, 1986, 16.

13. Ibid. Some of the land purchased by Watkins is still held by the North American Land Company, a descendant of the original London-based company.

14. Ibid.

15. Millet, "Economic Development of Southwest Louisiana."

16. Ibid.

17. Perrin, *Southwest Louisiana Historical and Biographical*, 140.

18. Millet, "Economic Development of Southwest Louisiana."

19. Ibid.

20. Dobson, *Guilty?* 8.

21. Ibid.

22. Ibid.

Chapter 5

1. Abstract of title in possession of current owner Genevieve LeBlanc.

2. Perrin, *Southwest Louisiana Historical and Biographical*, 160.

3. Fred is listed in Louisiana in the 1900 federal census but claimed he had gone back to Iowa by the time of the murders in February 1902. *Twelfth Census of the United States: Schedule No. 1—Population. Ward 2. Calcasieu Parish, LA, June* 20, 1900, B, sheet no. 11.

4. Dobson, *Guilty?* 8.

5. Jack Giovo, I. Bruce Turner, and Linda Parker Langley, *Jefferson Davis Parish: An Oral History* (Jennings: Jeff Davis Arts Council, 2000), 8.

6. Ibid.

7. Ibid.

8. Ibid.

9. A railroad section is a portion of the track maintained by a single crew. In southwest Louisiana each section consisted of five miles of track. The section house is the gathering and equipment storage place for the crew.

10. Jack Giovo et al., *Jefferson Davis Parish*, 8.

11. Perrin, *Southwest Louisiana Historical and Biographical*, 160.

12. Ibid. The *Crescent* was out of business by 1902 but had been supplanted by the *Welsh Rice Belt Journal*, which was established in 1900.

13. Perrin, *Southwest Louisiana Historical and Biographical*, 160.

14. U.S. Department of Commerce and Labor, Bureau of the Census, *Thirteenth Census of the United States, Population of Minor Civil Divisions, 1910, 1900 and 1880* (Washington, DC: Government Printing Office), Louisiana Table 1.

15. "May Be Earl Murderer," *New-York Tribune*, February 27, 1902, 5.

Chapter 6

1. "Batson in Prison Here," *New Orleans Picayune*, March 6, 1902, 1, 4.

2. For example, see "Batson in Prison Here," 4.

3. Ibid.

4. "Held For Murder," *Princeton (MO) Telegraph*, March 9, 1902, 1.

5. "Batson in Prison Here," 4.

6. "Held For Murder," 1.

7. Ibid.

8. Ibid.

9. Ibid.

10. "Batson's Tissue of Falsehoods," 2.

11. "Batson in Prison Here," 4.

12. "Swift Justice for Ed Batson," *Lake Charles Weekly American*, March 1, 1902, 5.

13. "Held for Murder," 1.

14. "Batson Again Faces Death," *Lake Charles Weekly American*, March 20, 1903, 2.

15. "What Batson Has to Say," *Lake Charles Weekly American*, March 1, 1902, 4.

16. "Batson in Prison Here," 4.

17. "In No Hurry to Come Back," *Lake Charles Weekly American*, March 8, 1902, 2.

18. Ibid., 2.

19. "What Batson Has to Say," 4.

20. Ibid.

21. "In No Hurry," 2.

22. Ibid.

23. "What Batson Has to Say," 4.

24. Ibid.

25. "The Oil Gusher Near Beaumont," *New Orleans Picayune*, January 16, 1901, 1.

26. Ibid.

27. Ibid.

28. "In No Hurry," 2.

29. Ibid.

30. Ibid.

31. Ibid.; "Batson Makes Detailed Statement," 1.

32. "Batson Makes Detailed Statement," 1.

33. Ibid.

34. Ibid.

35. "Batson's Tissue of Falsehoods," *Lake Charles Weekly American*, March 8, 1902, 2.

36. "The Earl Murder," *New Orleans Picayune*, March 1, 1902, 1.

Chapter 7

1. "Due at New Orleans Today," *Lake Charles Weekly American*, March 8, 1902, 5.

2. "Batson, the Butcher, to Be Brought Back," *New Orleans Picayune*, February 28, 1902, 1.

3. "Horrible & Gruesome Tragedy Near Welsh," 1.

4. "Batson in Prison Here," 4.

5. "Indignation at Welsh," *New Orleans Picayune*, February 28, 1902, 11.

6. Ibid.

7. Ibid.

8. "Landed Safe in New Orleans," *Lake Charles Weekly American*, March 8, 1902, 5.

9. Ibid.

10. *Twelfth Census of the United States: Schedule No. 1—Population. Morgan Township. Princeton City, Mercer County, MO, June 12, 1900*, 210 A, sheet no. 11.

11. "Landed Safe in New Orleans," 5.

12. "Batson in Prison Here," 1.

13. “Earl Murders under Review,” 5.

14. Ibid.

15. “Batson in Prison Here,” 1.

16. “Earl Murders under Review,” 5.

17. “Landed Safe in New Orleans,” 5.

18. “Earl Murders under Review,” 5.

19. Ibid.

20. “Batson in Prison Here,” 1.

21. “Earl Murders under Review,” 5.

Chapter 8

1. “Batson in Prison Here,” 4.

2. Ibid.

3. Ibid.

4. “Landed Safe in New Orleans,” 5.

5. Ibid.

6. “Batson in Prison Here,” 4.

7. Ibid.

8. Ibid.

9. Ibid. The studio of B & G Moses Photographers was supposed to be one of the best around, making it quite curious that the scar could be accidentally left in the photo. In 1902 the studio was operated by Gustave A. Moses. He and his brother, Bernard, who died in 1899, had been trained by their father, Samuel Moses, who opened the studio in 1849 after he and his family emigrated from Bavaria. “B. & G. Moses Photographers,” accessed January 27, 2014, http://www.amistadresearchcenter.org/archon/?=creators/creator&id=235.

10. Ibid.

11. Ibid.

12. Ibid.

13. “Batson’s Trial Will Be Delayed,” *New Orleans Picayune*, March 8, 1902, 12.

14. “Belief in Her Son Unshaken,” *Lake Charles Weekly American*, April 26, 1902, 5.

15. “Landed Safe in New Orleans,” 5.

16. “Due at New Orleans Today,” *Lake Charles Weekly American*, March 8, 1902, 5.

17. “Batson in Prison Here,” 1.

18. “Earl Murders under Review,” 5.

19. Ibid.

Chapter 9

1. "Man Who Helped Kill Earls Slain," *Washington (DC)Times*, February 28, 1902, 7.

2. Ibid.

3. Ibid.

4. "Horrible Massacre at Welsh," *Abbeville Meridional*, March 1, 1902, 2.

5. "Grand Jury to Meet Monday," *Lake Charles Weekly American*, March 15, 1902, 1.

6. "Fresh Evidence against Batson," *St. Louis Republic*, March 25, 1902, 9.

7. Ibid.

8. Ibid.

9. "Batson's Trial Will Be Delayed, *New Orleans Picayune*, March 8, 1902, 12.

10. Ibid.

11. "No Doubt of His Identity," *Lake Charles Weekly American*, March 15, 1902, 3.

12. "Batson Pays the Death Penalty," *New Orleans Picayune*, August 14, 1903, 8.

13. "Another Link in the Chain," *Lake Charles Weekly American*, March 15, 1902, 3.

14. Dobson, *Guilty?* 23.

15. "Another Link in the Chain," 3.

16. "Batson's Trial Will Be Delayed," 12.

17. Ibid.

18. Ibid. The gloves were never traced to Batson.

Chapter 10

1. "Nine-Year-Old Child Victim of Fiendish Crime," *Lake Charles Weekly American*, March 15, 1902, 1.

2. Ibid.

3. Nola Mae Ross, *Crimes of the Past in South Louisiana* (Lake Charles, LA: printed by author, 2004), 43.

4. Ibid., 44.

5. Ibid., 45.

6. Ibid., 41, 46.

7. "Grand Jury to Meet Monday," 1.

8. "Batson Tells His Story," *Lake Charles Weekly American*, March 22, 1902, 2.

9. "The Murder of Iris Kennedy," *Daily American*, April 21, 1908, 1.

10. Ibid.

Chapter 11

1. "Batson's Motion to Quash Is Overruled," *St. Louis Republic*, March 21, 1902, 2.

2. Donald J. Millet, ed., *Centennial History of Lake Charles, 1867–1967* (Lake Charles, LA: Lake Charles Letter Shop, 1967). Pages not numbered.

3. "City's Wild and Wooly Days Recalled by Local Historian," *Lake Charles American Press*, May 19, 1957, 12. Wooly is the spelling in the original.

4. Ibid.

5. Millet, *Centennial History of Lake Charles*.

6. Thomas Watson, "High Noon in Lake Charles: The Lyons-Woodlief Showdown," *Louisiana History* 51, no. 3 (2010): 333.

7. "Batson Held at Lafayette," *New Orleans Picayune*, March 19, 1902, 1.

8. "Batson's First Day in Court," *Lake Charles Weekly American*, March 22, 1902, 8.

9. Ibid., 8.

10. "Batson Held at Lafayette," 1.

11. "City's Wild and Wooly Days," 12. The jail was destroyed in the great Lake Charles fire in 1910 and rebuilt in 1911. It was finally torn down in 1956.

12. "Batson's First Day in Court," 8.

13. Ibid.

14. Ibid.

15. "Funeral Services for Judge Winston Overton Are Set for 4:30 Today," *Lake Charles American Press*, September 10, 1934, 1.

16. According to Sompayrac's obituary, he served as an assistant attorney general during the administrations of Luther E. Hall (1912–1916) and John M. Parker (1920–1924), and for several years was a law partner of Governor Hall's. "Assistant Attorney for Dock Board Dies," *New Orleans Times-Picayune*, November 25, 1933.

17. "Batson's First Day in Court," 8.

18. "'Not Guilty,' Says Batson," *Lake Charles Weekly American*, March 22, 1902, 1.

19. Ibid.

20. Ibid.

21. Ibid. It is not clear whether the date of February 12 was actually in the indictment or was a typographical error in the newspaper. All other accounts place the murder on February 13, even though the coroner was unable to swear to an exact time of death.

22. Ibid.

Chapter 12

1. Genealogy prepared by Pat William Chennault, Lawton, Oklahoma.

2. Ibid.

3. Ibid.

4. Ibid.

5. "Batson's Mother in Town," *Lake Charles Weekly American*, April 12, 1902, 4.

6. "Through His Mother's Eyes," *Lake Charles Weekly American*, April 19, 1902, 2.

7. "Batson's Mother in Town," 4.

8. "Through His Mother's Eyes," 2.

9. "Batson's Mother in Town," 4.

10. "Through His Mother's Eyes," 2.

11. Ibid.

12. Ibid.

13. Ibid.

14. Ibid.

Chapter 13

1. "Fail to Identify Him," *Jennings Daily Record*, March 12, 1902, 4.

2. Ibid.

3. Ibid.

4. Ibid.

5. Ibid.

6. Ibid.

7. "Maud Earll Visits Batson," *Grundy County (MO) Gazette*, April 16, 1902. This clipping is from Batson family documents and shows no page number.

8. Ibid.

9. Ibid.

10. "Crime of the Century," 7.

11. "Maud Earll Visits Batson."

12. Ibid.

13. Genealogy prepared by Pat William Chennault, Lawton, Oklahoma.

14. "Batson, the Butcher, To Be Brought Back," *New Orleans Picayune*, February 28, 1902, 1.

15. "Death Penalty for Ed Batson," 3; "Indignation at Welsh," *New Orleans Picayune*, February 28, 1902, 11; "Six Buried in One Grave," 8.

16. "The Earll Land Will Not Be Sold," *New Orleans Daily Picayune*, March 8, 1902, 12.

17. "Traced into Lake Charles," 1; "Death Penalty for Ed Batson," 3.

18. *Twelfth Census, Ward 2, Calcasieu Parish, LA*, B, sheet no. 11.

19. "Batson's Tissue of Falsehoods," 2; "Death Penalty for Ed Batson," 3.

20. "Fresh Evidence against Batson," 9.

Chapter 14

1. "Exchange Interviews," *Houston Daily Post*, April 19, 1902, 4.

2. Underwood, "The Other Batson Case," 794.

3. "State Wins Its First Point," *Lake Charles Weekly American*, April 19, 1902, 3.

4. Ibid.

5. Ibid.

6. "Traced into Lake Charles," 4.

7. "State Wins First Point," 3.

8. Ibid.

9. "Jury Completed Last Tuesday," *Lake Charles Weekly American*, April 19, 1902, 1, 8.

10. Underwood, "The Other Batson Case," 774.

11. "Jury Completed Last Tuesday," 8.

12. "The Crime of the Century," 7.

13. "The Pardon Board Gives Batson Chance for Life," *New Orleans Picayune*, July 28, 1903.

14. "Traced into Lake Charles," 4.

15. Ibid., 4.

16. Ibid.

17. Ibid.

18. Ibid.

19. Ibid. In the early 1900s, collars were detachable from shirts so that they could be starched while the shirt itself was not.

20. Ibid.

21. "Traced into Lake Charles," 4.

22. Ibid.

23. "Batson Pays the Death Penalty," 1.

24. "Traced into Lake Charles," 4.

25. Ibid.

26. Ibid.

27. Ibid.

28. Ibid.

29. Ibid.

30. "Another Link in the Chain," *Weekly American*, March 15, 1902, 3.

31. "Traced into Lake Charles," 4.
32. Ibid.
33. Ibid.
34. Ibid.
35. Ibid.
36. Ibid.
37. Ibid.

Chapter 15

1. "Death Penalty for Ed Batson," 3.
2. "Traced into Lake Charles," 4.
3. Ibid.
4. Ibid.
5. "Death Penalty for Ed Batson," 3.
6. Ibid.
7. Ibid.
8. Ibid.
9. Ibid.
10. Ibid.
11. Ibid.
12. Ibid.
13. Ibid. The newspaper report quotes Fred Earll as saying he came from Mount Eagle, Iowa, but there was no such place in 1902. He was said to be living in Eagle Grove, Iowa, at the time.
14. "Death Penalty for Ed Batson," 3. Kimble testified later that he recognized the gun and that it belonged to John or Fay Earll.
15. "Death Penalty for Ed Batson," 3. The Hampden Watch Company, formerly the New York Watch Co., moved to Springfield, Massachusetts, in 1877 and produced quality pocket watches until 1927.
16. "Death Penalty for Ed Batson," 3.
17. Ibid.
18. Underwood, "The Other Batson Trial," 776.
19. "Death Penalty for Ed Batson," 3.
20. Ibid.
21. "Alfred Batson Convicted of Murder In First Degree," *St. Louis Republic*, March 13, 1903, 2.
22. "Death Penalty for Ed Batson," 3.
23. Underwood, "The Other Batson Case," 778.
24. "Death Penalty for Ed Batson," 3.

25. Ibid.
26. Ibid.

Chapter 16

1. Underwood, "The Other Batson Case," 778.
2. "Death Penalty for Ed Batson," 3.
3. Ibid.
4. Ibid.
5. Ibid.
6. Ibid.
7. Ibid.
8. Ibid.
9. Ibid.
10. Ibid.
11. Dobson, *Guilty?* 45.
12. "Death Penalty for Ed Batson," 3.
13. "Edward Batson Convicted," *St. Louis Republic*, April 22, 1902, 14.
14. "Death Penalty for Ed Batson," 3.
15. Ibid.
16. Ibid.
17. Ibid.
18. Ibid.
19. Ibid.
20. Ibid.
21. "Marriage of Miss Maud Earl," *Lake Charles Weekly American*, April 26, 1902, 1.
22. "Batson Hears His Sentence," *Lake Charles Weekly American*, May 3, 1902, 2.
23. Ibid.

Chapter 17

1. Underwood, "The Other Batson Trial," 779.
2. "Confessed Killing the Earls," *Houston Daily Post*, April 27, 1902, 4.
3. "Man at Clinton, La. Says Batson Is Innocent of the Crime," *Jennings Daily Record*, April 26, 1902, 1.
4. Ibid.
5. Ibid.
6. "Trying to Get a New Trial for Batson," *Houston Daily Post*, June 6, 1902, 7.

7. *State v. Batson*, 32 So. 478, 108 La. 479 (1902). The Louisiana constitution that was in effect in 1902 called for a five-member supreme court, but it appears that only three judges heard the Batson case. Judge Frank A. Monroe wrote the majority opinion. Judge Joseph A. Breaux wrote a dissenting opinion. The third judge was probably Olivier O. Provosty, who was seated in 1901.

8. "Argued before Supreme Court," *Lake Charles Daily American*, June 8, 1902, 3.

9. *State*, 32 So. at 479, 483.

10. *State*, 32 So. at 480.

11. Underwood, "The Other Batson Trial," 780. The technicality addressed by the state supreme court had to do with admissibility of the note that allegedly had been attached to Ward Earll's door, and a legal document that was known to have been signed by Ward Earll. The prosecution attempted to prove that the signature on the note was not Ward Earll's by comparing it with the known signature on the legal document.

The majority of the court ruled the contract between Ward Earll and a land company "has no relevancy to the prosecution or the defense in this case" and that it was introduced only to establish a comparison between the signatures and that state law provided that "all crimes, offences, and misdemeanors shall be taken, intended and construed according to, and in conformity to, the common law of England." Early English cases prohibited "a direct comparison of handwriting" in instances such as the Batson case. The court held, "The writing offered to the jury in this case, and received by the court, for the purpose of instituting a comparison of handwriting only, was not admissible, and the defendant has been convicted upon illegal evidence. . . . It is ordered, adjudged, and decreed that the verdict and sentence . . . be set aside and annulled, and that this case be remanded to be proceeded with according to the law." *State*, 32 So. at 483.

12. *State*, 32 So. at 483.

13. "Gets Another Chance for Life," *Lake Charles Weekly American*, June 28, 1902, 2.

14. "Ed Batson to Be Tried Again," *Lake Charles Weekly American*, June 28, 1902, 1.

15. "New Evidence in Batson Case," *Lake Charles Weekly American*, September 27, 1902, 2.

16. Ibid. In fact, the parish was not building a completely new courthouse but substantially renovating and adding on to the old one.

17. "Batson a Changed Man," *Welsh Rice Belt Journal*, August 1, 1902, 1.

18. Ibid.

19. Ibid.

20. Ibid.

Chapter 18

1. “New Evidence in Batson Case,” 2.

2.”Can Batson Get Fair Play Here?” *Lake Charles Daily American*, December 11, 1903, 1.

3. “Refused to Grant Change of Venue,” *Lake Charles Daily American*, December 12, 1902, 1.

4. “Can Batson Get Fair Play Here?” 1.

5. Ibid.

6. “Refused to Grant Change of Venue,” 1.

7. Ibid.

8. “New Evidence in Batson Case,” 2. Armand J. Brinkhaus, an attorney and former state senator for many years in Louisiana, said: “I never heard of a defendant having to pay court costs because if convicted how do you get blood out of the turnip in jail and if acquitted, then he is scot free.” Armand J. Brinkhaus, e-mail message to Jim Bradshaw, November 25, 2012.

9. “Reappears the Amiable Batson,” *Lake Charles Weekly American*, March 13, 1903, 3.

10. “Reappears the Amiable Batson,” 3.

11. Ibid.

12. Ibid.

13. “Batson Found Guilty of Murder,” *Welsh Rice Belt Journal*, March 13, 1903, 8.

14. “Reappears the Amiable Batson,” 3.

15. “Batson Found Guilty of Murder,” 8.

16. “Reappears the Amiable Batson,” 3. Newspaper reports of the second trial did not give the hometowns of the jurors as they did in the first trial.

17. Ibid.

18. Ibid.

19. Ibid.

20. Ibid.

21. “Making Stories against Batson,” *Lake Charles Daily American*, March 11, 1903, 1.

22. “Reappears the Amiable Batson,” 2.

23. “Making Stories against Batson,” 1.

24. Ibid.

25. Ibid. Mardi Gras season is called Carnival in New Orleans.

26. “Batson Again Faces Death,” 2.

27. Ibid.

28. Ibid.

29. Ibid.

30. Ibid. According to Underwood, "The fact is that the loss of the vest would not have made testimony about the original vest and its contents inadmissible. The State would have had no reason to lose the vest or substitute another in its place, and today's lawyer would immediately shift gears and offer the 'substitute' as demonstrative evidence, as a vest like the one or similar to the one found in the buggy." Underwood, "The Other Batson Case," 783.

31. "Defense Offers Few Witnesses," 1.

32. "Batson Again Faces Death," 2.

33. "Defense Offers Few Witnesses," 1.

34. "Batson Again Faces Death," 2.

35. "Batson Fairly Dealt With," *Welsh Rice Belt Journal*, March 13, 1903, 1.

36. "Defense Offers Few Witnesses," 1.

37. Underwood, "The Other Batson Case," 785.

38. "Reappears the Amiable Batson," 3.

39. "Batson Again Faces Death," 2.

40. Ibid.

41. Ibid.

42. Ibid.

43. Ibid.

44. Ibid.

45. Ibid.

46. Ibid.

47. Ibid.

Chapter 19

1. "Batson Again Faces Death," 2.

2. Ibid.

3. Ibid.

4. Ibid.

5. Ibid.

6. Ibid.

7. Ibid.

8. "Batson Fairly Dealt With," 1.

9. "Batson Again Faces Death," 2.

10. "Batson Makes a Statement," *Welsh Rice Belt Journal*, March 20, 1903, 7. By *brant*, Batson was probably referring to the Canada goose (*Branta canadenis*), which until the 1950s was one of the first geese to arrive in Louisiana during the fall migration from the north. Most of them ended up on the prairies of southwest Louisiana, arriving in late September and

staying until late March, so they would have still been abundant, particularly in cutover rice fields in mid-February when the Earll murders took place. See George H. Lowry Jr., *Louisiana Birds* (Baton Rouge: Louisiana State University Press, 1974), 169.

11. "Batson Makes a Statement," 7.

12. "Death Sentence Passed on Two Men," *Lake Charles Daily American*, March 19, 1903, 1.

13. "Death Sentence Passed," 1.

14. Ibid.

Chapter 20

1. Dobson, *Guilty?* 5.

2. Dobson probably was not aware there was a story to go along with his theory of vengeance. In August 1845, Moses Earll, father of L. S. Earll, was one of several men charged with homicide after the shooting of deputy sheriff Osman N. Steele in Delaware County, New York, during the so-called Anti-Rent Riots. Steele was shot on Earll's farm when he tried to auction Earll's livestock because Earll owed $60 rent on his 160-acre farm. At the trial, six men, including Earll, were found guilty of murder. Four of them were sentenced to life in prison, two were sentenced to death. Those death sentences were commuted to life in prison when a new governor came into office, and in 1847 all the men were set free. See "Horrible Outrage and Murder," *Delaware County (NY) Gazette*, August 13, 1845; "Posse Captures Prisoners," *Delaware County (NY) Gazette*, August 20, 1845. The pages are not numbered.

3. Dobson, *Guilty?* 16–17.

4. Ibid., 17.

5. Ibid.

6. Ibid., 17, 18.

7. Ibid., 18–19.

8. Ibid., 19.

9. Ibid., 20.

10. Ibid., 20–21.

11. Ibid., 21.

12. Ibid., 21–22.

13. Ibid., 22–23.

14. "Inhuman Crime at Welsh," 1.

15. "No Doubt of His Identity," 3.

16. Dobson, *Guilty?* 22.

17. Ibid., 25, 26.

18. Ibid., 27–28.

19. Ibid., 29.

20. Ibid., 30–31, 32.

21. Ibid., 35. Something can be said about the place and time when the first brick building in Lake Charles was the jail and the second was the Lake City Saloon, which local historian Maude Reid described as "an ornate affair . . . with gilded mirrors, marble topped mahogany bars, and astonishing paintings." "City's Wild and Wooly Days," 12.

22. Dobson, *Guilty?* 36.

23. Ibid.

24. Underwood, "The Other Batson Case," 792.

25. Ibid., 38–39.

Chapter 21

1. "Lake Charles Thrown into a Wild Ferment," *New Orleans Picayune*, July 29, 1903, 1. Underwood noted that "having the trial judge sit on a committee reviewing the case for possible error or leniency seems a bit odd, but it appears to have been the established practice of the day." Underwood, "The Other Batson Case," 794.

2. "Formal Appeal for Clemency," *Lake Charles Daily American*, May 29, 1903, 3.

3. "Lake Charles Thrown into a Wild Ferment," 1.

4. Ibid.

5. "May Escape Death Penalty," *Welsh Rice Belt Journal*, July 31, 1903, 1.

6. "To Condemn Board of Pardons," *Lake Charles Daily American*, July 30, 1903, 1.

7. "May Escape Death Penalty," 1.

8. "The Pardon Board Gives Batson Chance," 8.

9. Ibid.

10. Ibid.

11. Ibid.

12. Ibid.

13. "Batson Still Has a Chance for Life," *Lake Charles Daily American*, July 28, 1903, 1.

14. "Batson Still Has a Chance," 1.

15. Ibid.

16. "Lake Charles Thrown into a Wild Ferment," 1.

17. Ibid.

18. "Protest from Lake Charles," *New Orleans Picayune*, July 30, 1903, 1.

19. Ibid.

20."To Condemn the Board of Pardons," 1. According to one report, the committee that drafted the resolution consisted of six members, another said it was made up of seven members.

21. Ibid.

22. "Governor Heard Should Follow Precedent," *Alexandria Louisiana Democrat*, August 5, 1903. This clipping has no page number.

23. "What Will the Lesson Be," *Lake Charles Daily American*, August 3, 1903, 2.

24. "Pelican State Opinions," *Lake Charles Daily American*, July 7, 1903, 2.

25. "Guion on Evidence," *Lake Charles Daily American*, July 29, 1903, 2.

26. "Protest from Lake Charles," 1; "Conferred with Judge Miller," *Lake Charles Daily American*, August 3, 1903, 1; "Batson Still Has a Chance for Life," 1.

27. "Protest from Lake Charles," 1.

28. Ibid.

29. "Lake Charles Thrown into a Wild Ferment"; "The Pardon Board Gives Batson Chance for Life."

30. "Batson to Hang," *Princeton (MO) Telegraph*, August 13, 1903, 1.

Chapter 22

1. "New Appeal to the Governor," *Lake Charles Daily American*, August 12, 1903, 1.

2. Ibid.

3. "Gov. Heard Firm in His Refusal," *Lake Charles Weekly American*, August 21, 1903, 2. According to Underwood, the women, Fans and Frazier, went to Baton Rouge with Rachel Payne. Underwood, "The Other Batson Case," 796.

4. "Unshaken on the Brink of Death," *Lake Charles Daily American*, August 13, 1903, 1.

5. "Batson's Lawyers Will Visit Governor Heard," *New Orleans Picayune*, August 13, 1903, 11.

6. "Gov. Heard Firm in His Refusal," 2.

7. "Batson Must Hang," *Welsh Rice Belt Journal*, August 14, 1903, 1. Heard served one term, from 1900 to 1904. It probably has no bearing on this case, but one of the notable achievements Heard is credited with is forming a state prison system and eliminating privately contracted prisons. Ed Batson was the first person legally executed during Heard's administration.

8. "Murderer Batson Will Hang Friday," *New Orleans Picayune*, August 11, 1903, 1.

9. Ibid.

10. "New Appeal to the Governor," 1.
11. "Murderer Batson Will Hang Friday," 1.
12. "New Appeal to the Governor," 1.
13. "Murderer Batson Will Hang Friday," 1.
14. "Gov. Heard Firm in His Refusal," 2.
15. "Batson Pays the Death Penalty," 1.
16. "New Appeal to the Governor," 1.
17. "Batson Pays the Death Penalty," 1.
18. "Batson Must Hang," 1.
19. "Batson Dies Next Friday," *Princeton (MO) Telegraph*, August 11, 1903, 1.
20. "Batson's Lawyers Will Visit Governor Heard," 11.
21. "Batson Must Hang," 1.
22. "New Appeal to the Governor," 1.

Chapter 23

1. Underwood, "The Other Batson Case," 797.
2. "Edward Batson's Plot to Escape Jail," *Abbeville Meridional*, November 1, 1902, 3.
3. "Batson Attempts Liberty," *Welsh Rice Belt Journal*, October 24, 1902, 1.
4. Ibid.
5. Ibid.
6. "Tender Sympathy for Batson," *Lafayette Advertiser*, November 8, 1902, 1.
7. Ibid.
8. Ibid.
9. "Batson to Hang," *Princeton (MO) Telegraph*, August 13, 1903, 1.
10. Ibid.
11. "Impudent Talk in Courtroom," *Lake Charles Weekly American*, August 14, 1903, 1.
12. "Batson's Lawyers Will Visit Governor Heard," 11.
13. "Unshaken on the Brink of Death," *Lake Charles Daily American*, August 13, 1903, 1.
14. Ibid.
15. "Batson's Death Warrant Signed," *Lake Charles Daily American*, June 12, 1903, 1.
16. "New Appeal to Governor," 1.
17. "Batson Pays the Death Penalty," 1.
18. "Unshaken on the Brink of Death," 1.
19. Ibid.
20. Ibid.

21. "Gov. Heard Firm in His Refusal," *Lake Charles Daily American*, August 14, 1903, 2.

22. "Kept His Lips Sealed," *Lake Charles Weekly American*, August 21, 1903, 3.

Chapter 24

1. "Batson Will Hang To-Day," *New Orleans Picayune*, August 14, 1903, 1.
2. "Batson Pays the Death Penalty," 1.
3. "Batson's Health Not Suffering," *Lake Charles Daily American*, May 14, 1903, 1. The title seems to be a contradiction of what the newspaper reported in this article.
4. "Kept His Lips Sealed," 3.
5. Ibid.
6. Ibid.
7. "Batson Pays the Death Penalty," 1.
8. Ibid.
9. "Unshaken on the Brink of Death," 1.
10. Ibid.
11. "Batson Will Hang To-Day," 1.
12. "Batson Pays the Death Penalty," 1.
13. "Kept His Lips Sealed," 3.
14. Ibid.
15. Ibid.
16. Ibid.
17. Ibid.
18. Ibid.
19. "Batson Pays the Death Penalty," 1.
20. Ibid.
21. "Kept His Lips Sealed," 3.
22. "Batson Pays the Death Penalty," 1.
23. Ibid.
24. "Kept His Lips Sealed," 3. Other witnesses mentioned in the newspaper story were deputy sheriffs D. C. Lyons, J. S. Caruthers, Isaac Fontenot, D. F. Foster, and C. B. Perkins, and witnesses J. W. Bryan, J. W. McFatter, J. C. LeBleu, J. T. Sanford, S. O. Shattuck, T. E. Price, M. Prentice, G. D. Moore, T. N. Hewitt, J. H. Hoffman, H. K. Welsh, and Joe Courtney.
25. Ibid.
26. Ibid.
27. "Batson Pays the Death Penalty," 1.
28. Ibid.

29. Ibid.

30. Ibid.

31. Ibid.

32. Ibid.

33. Ibid. Another account places the time at 1:43 P.M.

34. "Kept His Lips Sealed," 3.

35. "Batson Pays the Death Penalty," 1.

36. "Last Scene in Batson Tragedy," *Lake Charles Daily American*, August 13, 1903, 1.

37. Ibid.

38. Ibid.

39. Ibid.

40. Janet Batson Barney, Batson family genealogist, e-mail message to Danielle Miller, January 20, 2011.

41. "Batson Pays the Death Penalty," 1.

42. Barney, e-mail message to Danielle Miller, January 20, 2011. It is not clear why Rachel was in Seattle, but her grand-niece (granddaughter of Rachel's sister Susan), Leitha Mae Anderson, married Lewis Payne, the son of Joseph Payne and Harriett Dean in July 1903 in Grundy County, Missouri. They moved to Washington State after their first child, Roy Kenneth Payne, was born in 1904. Rachel may have been visiting or staying with them.

Afterword

1. The presumption of innocence has been upheld by the U.S. Supreme Court, which ruled in *Coffin v. United States*, 156 U.S. 432 (1895), "The principle that there is a presumption of innocence in favor of the accused is the undoubted law, axiomatic and elementary, and its enforcement lies at the foundation of our criminal law." *Coffin v. United States*, 156 U.S., 453.

2. The concept and phrase are included in a digest of Roman law compiled under the emperor Justinian I in the sixth century. See Kenneth Pennington, "Innocent Until Proven Guilty: The Origins of a Legal Maxim," accessed August 14, 2013, at http://faculty.cua.edu/pennington/Law508/InnocentGuilty.htm.

3. In the case of *In re Winship*, 397 U.S. 358 (1970), the U.S. Supreme Court firmly established that as a matter of due process a person charged with a criminal offense, including a juvenile, can be found guilty only after the prosecution has proven every element of the crime "beyond a reasonable doubt."

4. "Batson Pays the Death Penalty," 1.

5. *Witherspoon v. Illinois*, 391 U.S. 510 (1968).

6. Ibid.

7. Ibid.

8. Ibid.

9. Dobson, *Guilty?* 101.

10. "Crime of the Century," 1.

11. "Batson Pays the Death Penalty," 1; "Horrible & Gruesome Tragedy Near Welsh," 1.

12. Dobson, *Guilty?* 107–9. According to John Garst, who brought the Batson case to Richard Underwood's attention, Janet Batson Davidson, a Batson relative, said that she had heard from relatives that years after Ed Batson's execution a black man on his deathbed put an ad in the newspaper in Columbia, Missouri, saying that Batson was innocent, but nobody could find a copy of that ad. Underwood, "The Other Batson Case," 798.

Appendix B

1. "Reappears the Amiable Batson," 3.

2. Maude Reid, *Early Calcasieu Doctors 1850–1912* (Lake Charles, LA: First National Bank, 1969), 66–67.

3. "Death Penalty for Ed Batson," 6.

4. Reid, *Early Doctors of Lake Charles*, 58–61.

5. "Landed Safe in New Orleans," 5.

Appendix C

1. Lake Charles averages about fifty-six inches of rain per year, according to records maintained by the National Weather Service office there.

2. The Calcasieu Parish Courthouse was extensively remodeled between Ed Batson's first and second trials.

Appendix D

1. Joshua Clegg Caffery, "Bye-Bye Batson: Creativity, and Lake Charles' Great Blues Ballad" (paper, American Folklore Society, New Orleans, LA, October 2012). A *stavin' chain* was a chain used to wrap around barrels to hold them together while barrel staves were applied and was probably a tool used by black slaves. The Lomaxes found at least two other performers who used the name Stavin' Chain.

2. Joshua Clegg Caffery, "Bye-Bye Batson."

3. Ibid.

4. Ibid.

5. Ibid.

6. Ibid.

7. Ibid.

8. Ibid.

9. John and Alan Lomax, *Our Singing Country* (New York: Macmillan, 1941), 335.

Bibliography

Census Records

Twelfth Census of the United States: Schedule No. 1—Population. Morgan Township. Princeton City, Mercer County, MO, June 12, 1900, 210 A, sheet no. 11.

Twelfth Census of the United States: Schedule No. 1—Population. Ward 2. Calcasieu Parish, LA, June 20, 1900, B, sheet no. 11.

U.S. Department of Commerce and Labor, Bureau of the Census, *Thirteenth Census of the United States, Population of Minor Civil Divisions, 1910, 1900 and 1880* (Washington, DC: Government Printing Office), Louisiana Table 1.

Court Cases

In re Winship, 397 U.S. 358 (1970).

Supreme Court of Louisiana, *State v. Batson*, 32 So. 478, 108 La. 479 (1902).

U.S. Supreme Court, *Coffin v. United States*, 156 US 432 (1895).

U.S. Supreme Court, *Witherspoon v. Illinois*, 391 U.S. 510 (1968).

Journal Articles and Books

Arceneaux, William. *No Spark of Malice*. Baton Rouge: Louisiana State University Press, 1999.

Brackenridge, Henry M. *Views of Louisiana*. Pittsburgh, PA: Cramer, Spear, and Eichbaum, 1814.

Caffery, Joshua Clegg. "Bye-Bye Batson: Creativity, and Lake Charles' Great Blues Ballad." Paper, American Folklore Society, New Orleans, LA, October 2012.

Dobson, Charles. *Guilty? Side Lights on the Batson Case*. New Orleans: L. Graham Company, 1903.

Giovo, Jack, I. Bruce Turner, and Linda Parker Langley, *Jefferson Davis Parish: An Oral History*. Jennings, LA: Jeff Davis Arts Council, 2000.

Holmes, Walter C. *Flore Louisiane*. Lafayette, LA: Center for Louisiana Studies, 1990.

Lomax, John, and Alan Lomax. *Our Singing Country: Folk Songs and Ballads*. New York: Macmillan, 1941.

Lowry, George H., Jr. *Louisiana Birds*. Baton Rouge: Louisiana State University Press, 1974.

Millet, Donald, Sr., ed. *Centennial History of Lake Charles, 1867–1967*. Lake Charles, LA: Lake Charles Letter Shop, 1967.

Millet, Donald, Sr. "The Economic Development of Southwest Louisiana, 1865–1900." PhD diss., Department of History, Louisiana State University, 1964.

Perrin, William Henry. *Southwest Louisiana Historical and Biographical*. New Orleans: Gulf Publishing, 1891.

Reid, Maude. *Early Calcasieu Doctors 1850–1912*. Lake Charles, LA: First National Bank, 1969.

Ross, Nola Mae. *Crimes of the Past in South Louisiana*. Lake Charles, LA: printed by author, 2004.

Underwood, Richard H. "The Other Batson Case." *Legal Studies Forum* 31, no. 2 (2007): 765–800.

Watson, Thomas. "High Noon in Lake Charles: The Lyons-Woodlief Showdown." *Louisiana History* 51, no. 3 (2010): 333–42.

Newspapers

LOUISIANA

Abbeville Meridional

"Edward Batson's Plot to Escape Jail," November 1, 1902, 3.

"Horrible Massacre at Welsh," March 1, 1902, 2.

Alexandria Louisiana Democrat

"Governor Heard Should Follow Precedent," August 5, 1903 (no page number).

Crowley Signal

"Horrible & Gruesome Tragedy Near Welsh," March 1, 1902, 1.

Jennings Daily Record

"Batson Meets Death Unshaken," August 14, 1903, 1.

"Fail to Identify Him," March 12, 1902, 4.

"Man at Clinton, La. Says Batson Is Innocent of the Crime," April 26, 1902, 1.

Lafayette Advertiser
"Tender Sympathy for Batson," November 8, 1902, 1.

Lafayette Daily Advertiser
Bradshaw, Jim. "Batson murder trial was talk of parish in 1902," October 28, 1997, 1B.

Lake Charles American Press
"City's Wild and Wooly Days Recalled by Local Historian," May 19, 1957, 12.
"Funeral Services for Judge Winston Overton Are Set for 4:30 Today," September 10, 1934, 1.
Nola Mae Ross, "Gigantic Vision Drowned in Salty Water," April 20, 1986, 16.

Lake Charles Daily American
"A Remarkable Report," December 15, 1902, 2.
"Argued before Supreme Court," June 8, 1902, 3.
"Batson's Death Warrant Signed," June 12, 1903, 1.
"Batson's Health Not Suffering," May 14, 1903, 1.
"Batson Still Has a Chance for Life," July 28, 1903, 1.
"Can Batson Get Fair Play Here?" December 11, 1902, 1.
"Conferred with Judge Miller," August 3, 1903, 1.
"Court to Begin in February," December 31, 1902, 1.
"Death Sentence Passed On Two Men," May 19, 1903, 1.
"Formal Appeal for Clemency," May 29, 1903, 3.
"For Partition and Accounting," February 22, 1904, 4.
"Governor Says Batson Must Die," August 10, 1903, 1.
"Guion on Evidence," July 29, 1903, 2.
"Hearing Stories against Batson," March 10, 1903, 1.
"Heavy Work for the Courts," February 28, 1902, 4.
"Last Scene in Batson Tragedy," August 13, 1903, 1.
"Making Stories against Batson," March 11, 1903, 1.
"Mrs. Payne Arrives in Town," August 4, 1903, 1.
"New Appeal to the Governor," August 12, 1903, 1.
"New Evidence in Batson Case," September 19, 1902, 4.
"Pelican State Opinions," July 7, 1903, 2.
"Refused to Grant Change of Venue," December 12, 1902, 1.
"The Murder of Iris Kennedy," April 21, 1908, 1.
"The Pelican State," November 24, 1902, 2.
"To Argue for Change of Venue," November 10, 1902, 1.
"To Condemn the Board of Pardons," July 30, 1903, 1.
"Unshaken on the Brink of Death," August 13, 1903, 1.
"What Will the Lesson Be," August 3, 1903, 2.

Lake Charles Weekly American
"Another Link in the Chain," March 15, 1902, 3.
"Batson Again Faces Death," March 20, 1903, 2, 3, 6.
"Batson Case May Be Appealed," April 4, 1903, 1.
"Batson Hears His Sentence," May 3, 1902, 2.
"Batson Makes Detailed Statement," March 1, 1902, 1.
"Batson's First Day in Court," March 22, 1902, 8.
"Batson's Mother in Town," April 12, 1902, 4.
"Batson's Tissue of Falsehoods," March 8, 1902, 2.
"Batson Tells His Story," March 22, 1902, 2.
"Belief in Her Son Unshaken," April 26, 1902, 5.
"Death Penalty for Ed Batson," April 26, 1902, 3.
"Due at New Orleans Today," March 8, 1902, 5.
"Earl Murders Under Review," March 8, 1902, 5.
"Ed Batson to Be Tried Again," June 28, 1902, 1.
"Gets Another Chance for Life," June 28, 1902, 2.
"Gov. Heard Firm in His Refusal," August 21, 1903, 2.
"Grand Jury to Meet Monday," March 15, 1902, 1.
"Impudent Talk in Courtroom," August 14, 1903, 1.
"Inhuman Crime at Welsh," March 1, 1902, 1.
"In No Hurry to Come Back," March 8, 1902, 2.
"Jurors Who May Try Batson," March 29, 1902, 1.
"Jury Completed Last Tuesday," April 19, 1902, 1, 8.
"Kept His Lips Sealed," August 21, 1903, 3.
"Landed Safe in New Orleans," March 8, 1902, 5.
"Marriage of Miss Maud Earle," April 26, 1902, 1.
"New Evidence in Batson Case," September 27, 1902, 2.
"Nine-Year-Old Child Victim of Fiendish Crime," March 15, 1902, 1.
"No Doubt of His Identity," March 15, 1902, 3.
"'Not Guilty,' Says Batson," March 22, 1902, 1.
"Reappears the Amiable Batson," March 13, 1903, 3.
"Six Buried in One Grave," March 1, 1902, 8.
"State Wins Its First Point," April 19, 1902, 3.
"Swift Justice for Ed Batson," March 1, 1902, 5.
"The Crime of the Century," August 21, 1903, 1, 7.
"The Evidence in the Case," March 13, 1903, 5, 8.
"Through His Mother's Eyes," April 19, 1902, 2.
"Traced to Lake Charles," April 19, 1902, 1, 4, 5, 8.
"Two Days More of This World," August 14, 1903, 5.
"What Batson Has to Say," March 1, 1902, 4.

New Orleans Picayune
"Batson at the Bar of Justice," March 20, 1902, 1.
"Batson Held at Lafayette," March 19, 1902, 1.
"Batson in Prison Here," March 6, 1902, 1, 9.
"Batson Pays the Death Penalty for His Crime," August 15, 1903, 1.
"Batson's Case Has Not Yet Been Decided," August 1, 1903, 4.
"Batson's Lawyers Will Visit Governor Heard," August 13, 1903, 11.
"Batson's Trial Will Be Delayed," March 8, 1902, 12.
"Batson, the Butcher, to Be Brought Back," February 28, 1902, 1.
"Batson Will Hang To-Day," August 14, 1903, 1.
"Earll Family Murdered," February 25, 1902, 1.
"Indignation at Welsh," February 28, 1902, 11.
"Lake Charles Thrown into a Wild Ferment," July 29, 1903, 1.
"Murderer Batson Will Hang Friday," August 11, 1903, 1.
"Probably Done Late Thursday," February 25, 1902, 1
"Protest From Lake Charles," July 30, 1903, 1.
"The Earl Land Will Not Be Sold," March 8, 1902, 12.
"The Earl Murder," March 1, 1902, 1.
"The Oil Gusher Near Beaumont," January 16, 1901, 1.
"The Pardon Board Gives Batson Chance for Life," July 28, 1903, 8.

Welsh Rice Belt Journal
A. E. Bell & Company advertisement, June 27, 1902, page not numbered.
"Batson a Changed Man," August 1, 1902, 1.
"Batson Death Warrant Signed," June 19, 1903, 1.
"Batson Fairly Dealt With," March 13, 1903, 1.
"Batson Found Guilty of Murder," March 13, 1903, 8.
"Batson Gets New Trial," June 27, 1902, 1.
"Batson Makes a Statement," March 20, 1903, 7.
"Batson Must Hang," August 14, 1903, 1.
"May Escape Death Penalty," July 21, 1903, 1.

MISSOURI

Grundy County Gazette
"Batson Gets a New Trial," July 2, 1902, 1.
"Batson Hanged," August 14, 1903, 1.
"Ed Batson's Trial Has Been Postponed," October 1, 1902, 1.
"Maud Earll Visits Batson," April 16, 1902 (no page number shown).

Princeton Telegraph
"Batson Dies Next Friday," August 10, 1903, 1.
"Batson to Hang," August 13, 1903, 1.
"Held for Murder," March 9, 1902, 1.
"Paid the Penalty," August 19, 1903, 1.

St. Louis Republic
"Alfred Batson Convicted of Murder in First Degree," March 13, 1903, 2.
"Batson's Motion to Quash Overruled," March 21, 1902, 2.
"Batson Was Furious Over Damaging Testimony," March 22, 1902, 5.
"Edward Batson Convicted," April 22, 1902, 14.
"Fresh Evidence Against Batson," March 25, 1902, 9.

New York
Delaware County Gazette (no page number).
"Horrible Outrage and Murder," August 13, 1845.
"Posse Captures Prisoners," August 20, 1845.

New-York Tribune
"May Be Earl Murderer," February 22, 1902, 5.

TEXAS

Houston Post
"Batson Case with the Jury," April 20, 1902, 6.
"Batson Is Being Held," February 27, 1902, 3.
"Batson Is on Trial," April 15, 1902, 3.
"Change of Venue to Be Argued on Dec. 11," November 15, 1902, 8.
"Confessed Killing the Earls," April 27, 1902, 4.
"Exchange Interviews," April 19, 1902, 4.
"Trying to Get a New Trial for Batson," June 6, 1902, 7.

WASHINGTON, DC

Washington Times
"Earl Home Scene of Previous Murder," April 17, 1902, 1.
"Man Who Helped Kill Earls Slain," February 28, 1902, 7.

WEBSITES

"B. & G. Moses Photographers," accessed January 27, 2014, http://www.amistadresearchcenter.org/archon/?=creators/creator&id=235.

Index